Please Stop
Laughing at Me . . .

Please Stop
Laughing at Me . . .

One Woman's Inspirational Story

Jodee Blanco

Adams Media Corporation
Avon, Massachusetts

Published by
Adams Media Corporation
57 Littlefield Street, Avon, MA 02322 U.S.A.
www.adamsmedia.com

ISBN: 1-58062-836-2

Printed in the United States of America.

J   I   H   G   F   E   D   C   B   A

Library of Congress Cataloging-in-Publication Data
Blanco, Jodee.
Please stop laughing at me / Jodee Blanco.
p.   cm.
ISBN 1-58062-836-2
1. Bullying. I. Title.
BF637.B85 B57   2003
305.235'092--dc21   2002151475

This publication is designed to provide accurate and authoritative information
with regard to the subject matter covered. It is sold with the understanding that
the publisher is not engaged in rendering legal, accounting, or other professional
advice. If legal advice or other expert assistance is required, the services of a
competent professional person should be sought.
　　—From a *Declaration of Principles* jointly adopted by a Committee of the
American Bar Association and a Committee of Publishers and Associations

Many of the designations used by manufacturers and sellers to distinguish
their products are claimed as trademarks. Where those designations appear in
this book and Adams Media was aware of a trademark claim, the designations
have been printed with initial capital letters.

The following story is inspired by actual events. However, the names, places,
and dates have been changed to protect the privacy of those involved.

Excerpts from Edgar Lee Masters's *Spoon River Anthology* on page 133 are
from the University of Illinois Press edition, 1992.

*This book is available at quantity discounts for bulk purchases.
For information, call 1-800-872-5627.*

Contents

This book is a labor of love. It is dedicated to people who have cried themselves to sleep because they were "different." It is also a celebration of the "inner outcast" in all of us, and a humble attempt to inspire tolerance, understanding, and acceptance.

And to Niko . . . *Opou eisai, s'agapo mexri ta sinefa kai para pano.*

Acknowledgments

If it weren't for the following people, not only would the pages you're about to read never have been written, but this author would never have learned the real meaning of the words "to soar." The truth is, I would be nothing without the love and support of these people:

Kent Carroll, my dear friend and literary idol, who believed in me when I needed it more desperately than anyone could imagine. I'll never be able to express what you have done for me.

Jeff and Debbie Herman, my agents, advocates, and protectors extraordinaire. Your faith and encouragement are my oxygen.

Bob Adams and his remarkable team of caring professionals—Claire, Gary, Amy, Matthew, Kate, Paul, Sophie, Gene, Laura, Betty, Kristin, and everyone there who has believed in this book. I am forever grateful.

Lissy Peace, my soul sister, and the infinite source of sunlight in my life. Finally, a cheerleader thinks I'm cool!

Deena, you are my anchor.

Brondo, Shirley, and the Cavallo family. Knowing how

much you love me and that you were just a few miles down the road if I needed anything when I was up all night writing this book kept me sane. Words can't describe what you mean to me.

Zmuda, thanks for being my courage . . . and my precious friend.

Thomerson, Kinnison—you know who you are and why I love you so much. Enough said . . .

Candace Kent, Paul Dina, Bill Lindgren—you were there during those lonely, ugly years—now we are all swans— I adore you.

Everyone in Santorini—you breathed life into me, and have been filling me up ever since—*sas latrevo*.

The teachers who cared, especially Heleni Mitsus, Sister Rose Agatha, Mrs. Stencil, Mr. Palmer, Ms. Rudnik, Ms. Dudek, and "Waz." Every educator should be like you . . .

Dr. Damptz and Dr. Kirrin—for protecting me from myself.

"Deet"—for always being there.

Phil, you have given my heart a home. I could not have written this book without your love.

My grandparents, great aunts, and cousins. This book is a reality because you were there for me then . . . and now. I'm so proud that you're my family.

My parents, Joy and Tony Blanco. Mom, thank you for loving me, and for standing by my side when I was lonely and afraid. Daddy, I hope you are looking down from heaven and are proud of me. If I can be half the person you were, then I've really achieved something with my life.

Tiny, jagged hunks of mortar were being hurled at me from all sides. My hands over my face, I tried to run home, but the assault was too relentless. "Please stop," I pleaded. My knuckles and wrists were swollen and bloody. Red welts covered my skin. I didn't know what was worse, the physical or the emotional agony.

chapter one

Old Ghosts Come
Back to Haunt Me

High School Reunion

This is crazy. Why am I afraid? I'm behaving as if this is my first black-tie affair. Hell, I've hosted parties for heads of state. Not only do I often mingle and make interesting conversation with some truly important people, but I am frequently in charge of those events and under pressure to ensure that every detail goes smoothly. This event is nothing compared to those evenings.

Yet here I am, sitting in a rental car in a hotel parking lot in suburban Chicago where I grew up, scared to go to a party in my own hometown. I'm being ridiculous. It's just a high school reunion, there's nothing to be frightened of. They can't hurt me anymore. I'm successful now. I own a public relations firm. I travel widely and meet accomplished people. I work with famous authors and producers. I escaped those bullies at school. I'm finally living what I used to dream about as an adolescent when I listened to Barry Manilow's hit song "I Made It Through the Rain," the anthem of the ugly duckling turned swan.

Damn, who am I trying to fool? I'm terrified to get out of this car because I know inside the ballroom of that Hilton are ghosts from my past who still haunt me. When I second-guess myself at work, it isn't my own voice I hear in the back of my mind, it's the sound of my classmates from long ago—the very people who are now gathered less than one hundred feet away from me—laughing at me, beating me down. They destroyed my self-worth so much that it's taken me twenty years to stop hating myself.

If I walk through those banquet doors, is it possible that the confidence I've acquired since high school will dissolve into a puddle at my feet? What if who I am today—the life I'm leading now, with all its challenges and recognition—is just a pose? What if that terrified teenager I used to be, the outcast who came home with cuts and bruises, is still hiding inside me? Will she come out if one of the popular kids stares at me oddly or snickers? Will my confidence desert me when I see those familiar faces that caused me such pain? Will it hurt so badly that I'll revert back to that insecure person who couldn't stand to look in a mirror because she loathed who she saw?

What am I doing to myself? I'm not a teenager anymore. The people attending tonight's reunion are adults with children and jobs and grown-up lives. It's absurd to worry that they're going to gang up on me. I'm behaving like a neurotic twit. I've got to confront my fears. I'm not going to let memories of being bullied and picked on hold me hostage. I must get out of this car, walk across the parking lot, open those doors, and make an entrance. I must show everyone that I'm a sophisticated woman who doesn't even *remember* the events of high school, let alone allow herself to be affected by them.

When they see me, I bet their eyes will pop. No one expects me to attend. Or do they? Maybe they're curious to see what happened to the girl whose desperate pleas for acceptance kept them laughing semester after semester. Or worse, maybe they won't remember me at all.

A colleague at the University of Chicago had told me that the biggest problem with school bullying is mass denial. She explained that bullies don't realize the pain they're inflicting can cause lasting emotional and psychological scars. Society says "kids will be kids." As a result, the bullies get off the hook, and later don't recall hurting anyone, because in their minds, they were just being normal. Then they hear about a high school shooting, and are as shocked as everyone else that one student would kill another. Kids who are popular may observe bullying, but if it doesn't affect them, they don't pay any attention. Those who are truly aware are the people like me whose school years were hell— yet everyone thinks we're exaggerating the severity of what happened to us.

My hands are sweating. My head is fuzzy and confused. I'm biting my lip and it's starting to bleed. And look at my hair! They always made fun of my hair because it was so wavy and almost impossible to control. Tonight, it's wilder than ever. *Oh, God, I can't do this.* Why do I have to face yesterday's ghosts, anyway? I'm successful *today*.

A group of them just parked next to me. They see me sitting here. They're coming this way. I feel as if I've been transported back to the first day of my freshman year in high school . . .

chapter two

Trying to Soar
on Broken Wings

High School: First Day, Freshman Year

"Angel, come down and eat breakfast," my mom calls from downstairs.

"Mom, I'm too nervous to eat. Besides, I want my tummy to be super-flat. If I eat breakfast, I'll feel bloated. Just let me get dressed. I promise I'll eat a good lunch in the cafeteria," I respond.

"Jodee, I know you're scared that you won't fit in at Samuels, but this time it's going to be different. You'll make friends who share your interests. It's going to be a whole new world for you, honey," my mom says brightly.

I hope she's right. I yearn for acceptance. "Dear God," I pray over and over, "I'll do anything, just let the kids at Samuels like me. Please, don't let me be lonely anymore." I don't want my parents arguing about whose fault it is that their fourteen-year-old daughter is a social failure.

Junior high was rough. I tried to fit in, but I always felt as if a force field like the ones in those old 1950s science-fiction movies separated me from my peers. Each time I tried to penetrate the invisible wall between us, it repelled me, hurling me backward. I longed to be a part of the group. But the more I reached out to my classmates, the more they excluded me. They thought I was desperate.

I pledge not to make the same mistakes again. I swear to myself that I'll change—I'll even get into trouble once in a while if that's what it takes to make friends. Samuels is a jock school. "I'm not good at sports, but I can join the drama club and speech team," I confidently tell myself. The past is behind me. No more crying myself to sleep over the parties I don't get invited to, the cute boys who never speak to me, or the exciting secrets I'm never told.

Determined to make a positive impression, I wear my Vanderbilt designer jeans. They are so tight that I can barely breathe. My grandmother is right when she says beauty is pain. My mom has even bought me a pair of baby pink Candies to celebrate my first day. How I adore these shoes! They are clumsy, campy high-heel flip-flops, and I twist my ankle twice just breaking them in around the house. But all the popular girls are wearing them. If you want to be accepted, you wear Candies, and when I have them on, I feel beautiful and grown-up. Though they're only a pair of twenty-dollar strapless sandals, wearing them gives me the courage to face high school. My mother isn't crazy about the idea of her fourteen-year-old daughter in four-inch heels, but she is eager for me to fit in, and if the Candies help, I think she would purchase a truckload for me.

Bursting with hope and anticipation, I give myself one last inspection. Gazing at my reflection in the mirror, I can feel the old memories finally begin to recede. For the first time in years, I am not dreading the school day.

As the bright orange school bus pulls up to the corner, I hug my mom, grab my new school supplies, and rush out the door. I am floating on air. "High school will be different,"

I proclaim to myself. My dreams of dates and dances will be fulfilled. "Not only will I be accepted," I tell myself with near certainty as I board the bus, "I will be embraced by that mysterious, elusive society called the 'popular crowd.'"

I immediately recognize half the kids on the bus. Some of them are my neighbors. Others have gone to junior high with me. Even though I have spent the past four hours convincing myself that high school would be different, seeing these familiar faces and hearing them giggling and gossiping brings it all back. My insides go numb. I remember with alarming clarity what they used to do to me on the bus to junior high. All I want to do is turn around and go back home. Swallowing hard, I navigate my way to a seat.

Every school bus has a hierarchy, a caste system. The cool crowd—the kids who smoke, come to class with hickies, and get into just enough trouble to be the secret envy of the honor roll students—occupies the back rows. The cheerleaders and star athletes take the middle seats. The serious students sit near the front. The nerds and the outcasts never know where they'll end up. If they're lucky, they can find an empty seat directly behind or to the right of the driver.

As I make my way down the aisle, it becomes apparent that if I am going to get a seat, I will either have to fight or beg for it. Not anxious to do either, I decide to try reason. The cool crowd is too scary. The brains are too tight-knit a group to approach. So, I ask one of the cheerleaders, Nadia, who is often kind to me when no one else is around, if perhaps I could sit with her.

"Sorry, can't you see somebody's already sitting here?"

she responds, glancing over her shoulder to make sure her companions heard that she would never associate with someone who's not part of her clique.

"No, that's your *sweater* on the seat," I announce, gathering every ounce of courage I can muster.

"Better my sweater than you." With that, she and her friends explode into laughter. For a split second, she looks back guiltily, then quickly turns away.

The bus is crowded and, for a moment, I panic. The only seat available is at the very front, across from the driver. I bristle at the idea of starting my first day of high school in the "loser's seat." It's as if my fate is being sealed before I even step foot on school grounds. Clutching my bookbag, I move gingerly toward the front of the bus. It's like walking the plank to social oblivion.

As I settle into the small single seat opposite Mrs. Sullan, the driver, I feel a series of gentle tugs on my hair. I know if I glance over my shoulder, it will mean more laughter. So, as subtly as I can, I reach around and feel the back of my scalp, hoping that it's nothing more than a tiny insect caught in my hair. Moving my fingers through my mane, I nearly gag as I discover one spitball after another, thick and dripping with saliva. At least they're not whipping rocks at me like in junior high . . .

My eyes well with tears I don't dare shed. *Why must this happen?* I imagine the freshman year of my fantasies: the captain of the football team smiles at me by the lockers and asks for my phone number; the popular girl every guy in school wants to date runs up to me in between classes to see if I'd like to study at her house tonight. As I drift off into the security of my daydream, I am jarred awake by the sudden lurch of the bus as it pulls up in front of Samuels. While students file out into the parking lot, chattering and laughing, sharing stories of their summer escapades and back-to-school woes, I remain glued to the bus seat. How will I ever fit in? The last time I felt this anxious about starting a new school was the first day of sixth grade. I ignored my instincts, and ended up walking smack-dab into disaster. Could the same thing be happening all over again? Maybe I should pay attention to my fears this morning and get the hell out of here.

"Honey, don't let them get you down," Mrs. Sullan says reassuringly. "They're just being teenagers. They call me a worthless old widow when I catch them smoking and make them put out their cigarettes. My husband died of lung cancer. If these youngsters want to destroy their health, they're not going to do it on this school bus."

"I'm sorry, Mrs. Sullan," I respond, feeling sorry for her but not reassured.

"It's okay, dear. Go on into school. Show them all what you're made of," she urges me.

As I walk through the doors to the main building, I'm unable to get Mrs. Sullan out of my mind. I don't understand how kids can be so rude to such a nice woman. If they are angry with her for ruining their fun and they call her an old stick-in-the-mud, it would be disrespectful, but it wouldn't be cruel. But here is a woman who has to drive a bus to make ends meet, and these kids don't care what they say to her or how it hurts.

As I step inside Samuels's main building, the incident

on the bus recedes from my mind. Searching for my locker, I realize I have never before seen so many cute older boys in one place. Like my favorite disco song, it seems to be "raining men" all around me. Samuels is alive with energy. A group of cheerleaders, set apart from the rest of us in bright blue-and-gold school sweaters and short skirts, runs past me, joking and flirting with several of the football players. Couples are nuzzling each other in the halls, their sighs and giggles filling my head with fantasies of Saturday night dates and French kisses. I can hear locker doors clanging; students laughing and shouting across the hall to each other as they make their way to class; and the reverberating echo of the bell, signaling that it's time for first period. My ears soak up these wonderful sounds, for they are the music of my new beginning.

My first class is Public Speaking One. After completing roll call, our teacher, Mrs. Adams, a plump, warm-hearted woman in her late fifties with graying hair and a no-nonsense approach to education, enthusiastically describes what she'd like us to do this morning. "I'd like each of you to get up in front of the class and give an impromptu speech about any subject that interests you," she explains.

There is an audible groan in the room. She calls on us alphabetically. The only person whose last name comes before mine is absent. Just my luck. I have always loved talking in front of an audience, and I won first place in a state competition in junior high. But what if I'm the only one in this class who likes public speaking? If I go first and do well I'll be labeled "teacher's pet," and that will end my chances of making any friends in speech class. But if I do badly on purpose, I'll only be hurting myself.

"It looks like our first speaker will be Jodee Blanco," announces Mrs. Adams.

If you're good at something the popular crowd deems "uncool," you are sunk. I am frozen. I promised myself just this morning that I wasn't going to repeat old mistakes. Perhaps getting a low grade in speech class is a small enough price to pay to avoid the risk of being ridiculed and excluded. "After all, one C or a D isn't going to ruin my future," I say to myself without conviction. In the long run, one bad grade doesn't mean anything. But in the short term, I can't bear starting out every day of freshman year as the outcast of speech class. My decision made, I ready myself for my first test in cool.

"What subject have you chosen, dear?" asks Mrs. Adams, smiling broadly. When I don't respond right away, she says, "Jodee, is something wrong? I've heard from your eighth grade teacher that you're a *wonderful* speaker. Didn't you take first place in the state competition last year?"

Icy laughter ripples through the room. Seconds slowly pass. There is nothing I can do now—I'm busted.

"No, Mrs. Adams, I'm fine," I lie, trying to ignore the knot in my throat. "My topic is 'the Underdog,'" something I've thought about many times.

My hands sweat. My legs threaten to go out from under me. I pray for a fire drill, anything to get me out of this dilemma. A person should experience a nervous reaction if she is worried about failing, not because she's scared of succeeding. Taking a deep breath, I look out across the room, and begin.

Hello. My name is Jodee Blanco, and I'm going to share with you a story about an underdog—someone who everyone made fun of, someone who never got invited to parties, and who was so lonely, she felt lost. This girl had wild, wiry hair that never looked as if it was combed. She wasn't like the other kids at school. She would rather write poems and make up songs than hang out and talk about boys. She ached to have friends, but wasn't interested in the same things as her peers. They thought she was weird. They disliked the way she dressed. They didn't understand why she was different, and they chose not to try. Rather than opening their hearts to this strange, beautiful bird, she was cast out from the flock. She didn't fit in. As the years passed and the rejection she endured in school became buried in a secret place in her memory, she discovered she had a gift for turning those songs she used to hear inside her head into music that reached people's souls. Millions of people.

That misfit who everyone picked on, who was the butt of every joke and the target of so much cruelty, was Janis Joplin. You all know her music. It helped define a generation. Your children will listen to Janis Joplin, just as your parents did, and as I bet many of you do, too. Janis Joplin died in her twenties from a drug overdose. She was so full of pain and hurt that she tried to numb it with drugs. Eventually, they killed her. I'll always wonder: If the kids in her school had tried to get to know her, and instead of ridiculing and shunning her for being different, had embraced her for being special, would she still be alive today? We'll never know. But one thing we *do know for sure. There are people just like Janis Joplin among us now. Maybe that guy with the glasses who you make fun of at lunch will be the next Steven Spielberg or the next Elton John. The chubby girl with acne who you snicker at during gym class could be the next Bette Midler. They could also end up being so damaged from loneliness, so frustrated and sad, that they go through life never being all they could have. What you should understand is that to the underdogs at this school, some of you are like royalty. You're important. Your acceptance would mean so much. Next time you think of laughing at someone, stop for a second and think of Janis Joplin. Thanks for listening.* ■

Everyone stares at me as I take my seat. I can't read their reaction. Did they like my speech, or am I in for it after class?

"Jodee, that was wonderful. Just excellent," gushes Mrs. Adams. "Class, any comments?"

No one raises his or her hand. Giggles echo from the back rows. I want to crawl under my desk and disappear. The cheerleader sitting next to me hands me a note. Hesitantly, I open it.

YOU SUCK BITCH

Seeing these words scrawled in thick black ink triggers all the old fears. Familiar voices from grammar school bombard my memory. I can hear them chanting over and over in the schoolyard. *We all hate you, freak.*

Well, screw all of them, then and now! I didn't do anything

wrong. Though I try to be defiant and strong on the outside, inside, I am a mess. *Idiot, idiot, idiot! You should have followed your instincts and given a lousy speech, or at least talked about something neutral.*

Finally, the bell rings. First period is over. I gather my books. As I'm rushing out the door, Mrs. Adams stops me. "How would you like to join the speech team?" she asks, full of enthusiasm. "We'd love to have you. It's only a few people, but you'll enjoy yourself and learn a lot."

"Of course I'll join," I respond, allowing myself to feel hope again.

"Practice is every Wednesday night in the small theater."

"I'll be there!"

As I walk to my next class, I hear someone shouting my name. "Jodee, wait up," calls a female voice. I turn around and see one of the girls from speech class approaching me. Overweight with stringy hair, she has the posture of someone who carries a burden. Her eyes, though sad with deep shadows underneath, are the most arresting shade of green I've ever seen. They look like emeralds.

"Hi, I'm Noreen," she says softly, almost like a puppy that has been kicked so many times that it now expects rejection.

"Hi! By the way, you have the most amazing eyes. You ought to wear makeup to show them off better," I tell Noreen, grateful for her kindness.

The look on her face touches me. She fidgets with her notebook, unsure of how to respond to my compliment. "Really?" she whispers. "Thank you. I've never worn makeup. There just doesn't seem to be any point to it. No one ever cares how I look anyway." She seems relieved to have someone to talk to, embarrassed by what she has admitted.

"Do you want to go to the mall?" I ask. "We could go to Marshall Field's and experiment at the cosmetic counter."

"Wow, that would be great! I'd love to. By the way, I wanted to tell you that I thought your speech was wonderful. You were talking about me," she observes sheepishly.

"No," I reply. "I was talking about both of us."

Confirming plans to go shopping together Friday after school, we exchange phone numbers and dash to our next class. I make a quick stop at the lavatory. As I open the door and step inside, I cringe. The bathroom reeks of cigarette smoke and pot. There are no windows inside and the ventilation is poor. The smoke has nowhere to escape, so it visibly hovers beneath the fluorescent lights and makes my eyes burn.

Pulling my cosmetic case out of my purse, I hastily freshen my face. As I'm about to leave, a group of girls walks in. They look like a million dollars. Dressed in tight jeans, their hair perfectly feathered, and their makeup seamlessly applied, they are sharing intimate secrets about sex and boys and romantic fantasies about rock stars. I listen, fascinated, drawn to their conversation and longing to be a part of it. I linger, pretending that I'm rummaging through my bookbag for a tube of lip-gloss. Perhaps one of them will start a conversation with me, or I'll find the guts to talk to them.

One of the girls, Sharon, a tall blond with a reputation for toughness and daring, is in my history class. She is already one of the most popular girls in the freshman class. In junior high, everyone wanted to be like her. Most of her junior high classmates are at Samuels now, and her popularity has carried over. She approaches me.

"Hey, you're Jodee, right?" she asks, her voice guarded.

"Yes, Jodee Blanco," I respond, trying to sound composed. Sharon's clique is important. I know I am being tested and I feel my body tense. I don't want to make a mistake. I want these girls to like me.

"You're in my history class," she observes.

"Yeah, fourth period," I reply.

"Where did you go to junior high?" she inquires.

"I went to Northwest. Didn't you go to Northeast?" I ask, nonchalantly, determined not to let her see that I know who she is, and even worse, that she intimidates me.

"Yeah, Northeast was pretty cool," she reflects. Then, drawing a Marlboro out of her pocket and lighting it, she begins blowing smoke rings into the mirror. Her companions soon follow suit. One of them passes me her cigarette. I'm uncomfortable. They've opened the door and I don't want to close it, but I've never smoked before. The idea of taking a drag on a cigarette sickens me, but if I don't do it, won't it hurt my chances of being accepted?

"Hey, I may be getting a cold, and I don't want you guys to get sick," I blurt out, pleased with my quick thinking.

"That's cool," Sharon responds. The bell rings. "See ya," she calls out as she and her friends scurry to their next class. I let out a deep breath, relief flooding through me.

The afternoon is nearly over. I feel good. High school will be fine. One more period left today, biology. The teacher, Ms.

Raine, is a kind-hearted gnome of a woman. Her eyes twinkle when she smiles. She beams as she watches us pile into the lab. She is clearly an educator who adores her job. As we settle into our seats, I recognize several familiar faces from junior high. I can't catch my breath. "Roll call," announces Ms. Raine cheerfully. *The nightmare must not begin again.*

Tyler, who is sitting in front of me, rides the same school bus as I do. I've also seen him hanging around with some of the guys in my neighborhood. I have a huge crush on him. Ms. Raine passes by my desk and asks me to pick a name out of the jar for my lab partner. "Oh, please, God," I pray, "let it be Tyler's name." I close my eyes and wish as hard as I can as I hand the piece of paper I chose to Ms. Raine.

"Julie, you and Jodee will be lab partners this semester," she announces. "That's okay," I console myself. At least Tyler will be sitting at the desk directly in front of me all year.

A maverick, Tyler despises authority. It makes him irritating to teachers but irresistible to girls. He's wearing his typical outfit, a renegade's uniform: faded jeans, a concert T-shirt, a faded black cowboy hat, black cowboy boots, and a black leather jacket. A pack of Salems peeks out from his breast pocket. The teachers have struck a tacit bargain with Tyler. They let him dress as he wishes, as long as he doesn't disrupt their class. He has a strong sexual energy, with sensual brown eyes and long hair. I fantasize about him, yet fear him at the same time. My fear will be well founded, a kind of fear I first experienced when I was ten years old and in the fourth grade.

chapter three

Rainbows Lost

Fourth Grade

My great-aunt Evie, my grandmother's sister and my god-mother, was watching me that morning. It was my ninth birthday, and she wanted everything to be perfect. She and my grandmother were fussing about the house, arranging place settings, carefully placing candles in the enormous vanilla cake my mother had made the evening before, stringing brightly colored decorations and balloons through-out the dining room and kitchen, creating a festive circus of colors and images.

Aunt Evie was a large woman with huge, soft arms and a generous stomach. Often I would curl up and lay my head across Evie's abdomen, and listen, fascinated, as she enter-tained me with "Stoogie stories." I adored the Three Stooges, and would watch their old shorts on television. Evie would make up adventures featuring Moe, Larry, and Curly. It was astounding how she could weave these sponta-neous yarns. As she spun these wonderful original stories about my favorite television characters, she gently stroked my forehead, waiting for me to grow sleepy. She, her sisters, and my maternal grandmother were my constant protectors and companions. They taught me how to play poker, row a boat, shoot craps, and win at bingo. Odd tutelage for a child, but evidence that they loved me utterly.

That morning, my grandmother, Evie, and seven aunts had come over to help out at my birthday party. I was so excited. My classmates would be arriving in just a couple of hours.

Though my aunts were a generation older than my mom, they were more free-spirited than she. My mom was serious most of the time, while my aunts were eccentric and fun. When my grandmother was young, she and her sisters drank in speakeasies and hung out with stuntmen and bootleggers. They were progressive throughout their lives. They nurtured my silly, playful side.

"Jodee, let me fix your ponytail," my grandmother called from the kitchen.

"Okay, I'm coming," I responded, bounding down the stairs from my room.

"Don't run, you'll trip and fall," cautioned Evie.

"Oh, for God's sakes, Eve," chastised my Aunt Judy. "The kid's not a china doll."

Such was the atmosphere that day. My grandmother and my aunts, each in their own way, were doting on the birthday girl.

As my grandmother brushed my hair, I heard the back door open, the sound of shopping bags rustling, and my mom's high heels clicking across the kitchen floor.

"Mom, why can't daddy be here? Couldn't he have come back from his trip just one day early?" I asked, trying to hide my disappointment.

"Honey, you know daddy loves you with all his heart, but he's in Japan on business. You have all of us today. He'll be home next week," she said reassuringly.

"All right," I said, mustering as much enthusiasm as I could. Even though I knew my father was far away, I kept looking out the front window, thinking he might surprise me by showing up. Every time I peeked through those living-room curtains, my mom and aunts thought I was anxious for my party to start and was just checking to see if my friends had arrived.

My grandmother and aunts might have been my anchors, but my dad was my wings. He made me believe that nothing was impossible; you could achieve anything as long as you engaged your heart in the effort. He knew first-hand. Born and raised in New York City, he came from poverty. His parents, who died years before I was born, had owned a small cigar shop. By the time my father was sixteen, he was on his own, working eighteen-hour days in the mailroom of a large international shipping corporation. Within five years, he had advanced to junior vice president. My father captivated people. Tall and dark, he had black hair and warm, inviting brown eyes. Women adored him and men wanted to be his friend. He had a way of making someone feel as if he or she were the most important person in the world to him. Whether he was sharing beers with dockhands or clinking champagne glasses with CEOs, my dad was at ease with people no matter what they did or who they were.

A ham at heart, he bought a karaoke machine on one of his trips to Japan, long before the let's-pretend-we're-onstage device had been introduced into the American marketplace. He was a generous and imaginative host. Our home was always full of laughter, with friends and family frequently popping in and out. When my parents threw a party, my dad relished making each guest feel as if he or she was the center of attention. I adored my father. I could always talk to him. He never judged me. He and my mom raised me to come to them with any problems, and said that I should never be afraid to confide in them, regardless of the circumstances. Both Catholic, they instilled in me a strong sense of right and wrong. They taught me to be compassionate and tolerant, and to reach out to the underdog. My mom and dad also encouraged me to act independently, and to have a mind of my own.

My mom was supportive of my dad. Though he was often away from home on business, she rarely complained. She also worked in his office a few days a week, a comforting presence and helper. My parents had a loving marriage. Their friends enjoyed being around them. It was as if they gave off a glow, and others wanted to share their light.

As the morning slipped into afternoon, and the start of my birthday party loomed closer, I was beginning to realize that my dad was not going to surprise me as I had been hoping. "That's all right," I reassured myself. "Mom will take a lot of photographs, and on the weekend I can show them to him." The doorbell rang, awakening me from my daydream about my dad's return from Japan.

"Jodee, your friends are here," Evie sang out as she grabbed an enormous stack of party hats, and rushed to open the door and let in the flood of fourth graders.

"Coming," I yelled, thoughts of my dad receding, as I welcomed my classmates, their arms full of presents.

It was turning out to be a perfect day. My aunts were in

their glory, surrounded by giggling children digging their fingers into the delicious sugary concoctions that had been placed on each of their *Sesame Street* party plates. We played Pin the Tail on the Donkey. My Aunt Judy climbed a ladder to hang up an enormous piñata. My mom was holding her breath, afraid that Aunt Judy, who wasn't known for her grace, was going to tumble off those wobbly rungs at any second. The more the ladder shook, the harder we laughed. It was a magical day. We all took turns trying to break the piñata. Finally, Eddie, my favorite boy at school, whacked it so hard that candy scattered across the room. Within seconds, our French poodle, Shu Shu, and my grandmother's toy poodle, Toya, came barreling into the room, devouring the candy that had spilled across the floor. Everyone was laughing to the point of tears. My grandmother was snapping photographs and my mom had the 16-millimeter movie camera out, recording our excitement from every possible angle.

My mom knew that I was lonely as an only child. She was determined to help me have a wonderful birthday party, and she was so pleased when all my classmates arrived. But something made her hold back during the party—she seemed distant. Mom was like that sometimes: warm and affectionate one minute, stern and rigid the next. I think it was difficult for her to have only one child. I was more like a miniature adult to her.

My mom looked beautiful that day. With dark curly hair and magnetic hazel eyes, she turned heads everywhere she went. She believed that a woman should care about her appearance, and she taught me the same self-respect. My friends often told me that they wished their moms were as pretty as mine. Sometimes I wished my mom wasn't so conscious of how she looked. It would haunt me years later.

My classmates were having a wonderful time. I felt safe and happy. All my friends from school had come because they wanted to be with me on my birthday . . .

I was popular that year. At school, kids fought to sit next to me. We shared secrets. We even had our own made-up language that we used when we didn't want the grown-ups to understand what we were saying to each other. Our fourth grade teacher, Mrs. Stence, God bless her, was so patient with all of us. School was a dream. I enjoyed participating in class. My classmates thought I was brave and wise. They looked up to me.

I attended Holy Ascension, a Catholic grammar school where most of the teachers were nuns. My favorite was Sister Rose, a kind, gracious woman in her late sixties who treated us with sensitivity and warmth. My mom was fond of her as well. She was always giving me little presents for Sister Rose—small items to let her know how much she was appreciated.

My school had a special program for the deaf. One of the little girls enrolled in the program, Marianne, touched my heart every time I passed her in the hallway. Five years old, she had a clubfoot and wore heavy, clumsy-looking black shoes that had to be custom made to accommodate her deformity. Completely deaf, she was also vision impaired and wore thick glasses that seemed enormous on her tiny face. Because she was always dressed in raggedy hand-me-downs, some of the older students would snicker at her. They'd make fun of how she walked and her attempts to speak. Although she was five years old, only four years younger than me, I felt motherly instincts toward this little girl. I wanted to wrap my arms around her and make her feel loved. She had the most beautiful smile I'd ever seen.

I asked Sister Rose if I could volunteer as an assistant for the deaf program during my lunch hour. She immediately arranged it for me. Every day, I played with these remarkable kids, and helped Sister Clara—the cherubic young nun in charge of the program—teach them how to read lips. I would talk to them, and they would try to decipher what I was saying. I doted on Marianne. She seemed so alone in the world. Even some of the other deaf children shunned her.

One afternoon, I asked Sister Clara if I could bring Marianne to my house to play. "Please, Sister," I begged. "My mom said she would call Marianne's mom to make sure it was okay, and she'll pick her up and drop her off. Please!"

"I'll have to call Marianne's mother first," Sister Clara responded, walking to her office to make the call. A few moments later, she returned, smiling. "It's all arranged. I've got directions to her house. If your mom and you could pick her up on Saturday at eleven, that would be terrific." I was so excited, I thought I might burst.

Saturday morning, I was out of bed and dressed by 6:00 A.M. I made sure everyone else was up, too. My mom was looking forward to meeting Marianne. "Mom, where does she live? Is it far from here?" I asked.

"Yes, honey, it's about forty minutes away," she answered. As we neared Marianne's neighborhood, I began to notice that the houses seemed neglected.

"Mom, what's wrong, why do these houses look so sad?" I asked, not understanding why some of them had chipped paint and broken fences.

"Jodee, the people in this neighborhood are not as fortunate as we are. They don't have much money. You can say a prayer asking God to give them strength and opportunity," she said sadly.

Finally we pulled up in front of Marianne's house, a small bungalow. Though the home was in need of repair, the yard was well tended. You could see that Marianne's family, though they may have been poor, had dignity and self-respect.

As we approached the porch, a plump young woman with strawberry blond hair and kind eyes, opened the front door, smiling. "Hello! I'm Sherry, Marianne's mom. I can't thank you enough for inviting her out for the day. I worry that she's lonely, and I'm so busy with the new baby, I can't give her enough attention. She's timid and has trouble making friends in the program at school. This is the first time anyone has ever invited her over," she said, her eyes welling with tears.

"Jodee raves about your daughter, Sherry. I've been looking forward to finally meeting her," my mom replied.

"Thank you. Please come in and sit down."

The inside of the house, like the garden, was immaculate.

Though the furniture was old and worn and the living room decorated simply, it was neat as a pin. It was clear that Marianne came from a family who took pride in what little they had, and weren't ashamed of their limited circumstances.

Marianne and I had a wonderful afternoon together. Mom took us out for pizza and to the park, where we played for hours. Marianne was the little sister I had always fantasized about. She needed me and I her. I loved playing big sister and watching out for her. The other children in the park stared at us. When we passed them near the swings, they stepped back, almost as if they were afraid. My mom didn't want to embarrass Marianne and me or make a scene, so she gently took our hands, and together we got into the car and left.

"Mom, why were those kids in the park acting like that?" I asked as we drove home.

"Sometimes people are frightened by anyone who is different from them," my mother explained, speaking slowly to make sure I understood every word she said. "It doesn't mean they're bad people, just small-minded. Learn to ignore them. Marianne is your friend. Don't let anyone take that away from you."

"I know, mom," I replied, wishing I could erase the memory of being stared at.

Monday morning, as I rushed to Sister Rose's class, my best friend, Jo Ellen, stopped me in the hall. "I heard you were playing in the park with the retard," she said accusingly. "My sister saw you by the swings."

"Marianne is *not* a retard," I retorted. "She's handicapped."

"If you play with her, we can't play together anymore," stated the girl who I thought was my other half. "Marianne is creepy. If you spend time with her, you're creepy, too."

I considered Jo Ellen's ultimatum. She was my closest pal. We did everything together. Was Marianne worth it? I couldn't talk to her like I could talk to Jo Ellen. She was younger than me, and it was difficult to communicate with her because of her deafness. She was my pretend little sister, but I still needed a real best friend. How could I face school without one?

"Okay, Jo Ellen. I won't play with Marianne anymore. Please stay my best friend," I pleaded. The look of triumph on Jo Ellen's face told me that I had won her back. It was Marianne's face I was worried about. How could I look this little girl in the eye and tell her that I couldn't spend time with her anymore? "I don't have a choice," I convinced myself.

That afternoon, I told Sister Clara that I couldn't be a volunteer any longer.

"My mom wants me to come home for lunch for a while," I lied. "She says she doesn't think it's healthy that I don't get a break all day."

"All right, Jodee, I understand," Sister Clara replied, the disappointment in her voice cutting through me. She added, "The children will miss you, especially Marianne. She's grown so fond of you."

"I'm sorry, Sister, but my mom won't let me," I choked. With that, I ran out of the classroom. I noticed Marianne at the end of the hall coming in from recess. She saw me and smiled. She started to walk toward me. I pretended I didn't see her, and ran down the other end of the hall. I wanted to die. How could I do this? What was wrong with me? For weeks, I avoided being anywhere near the wing of the school where the program for the deaf was located. I was too ashamed to tell my mother what I had done, and I didn't want Sister Clara to know I had lied. My only solution was to hide. Every day at lunchtime, I would sneak into the girl's bathroom and hide behind the stalls. It would be an omen of events to come.

Then one day when I got home from school, my mom and dad were waiting for me in the living room. Daddy never came home during the day unless something was seriously wrong.

"Sister Clara called and asked me to reconsider my decision to not allow you to volunteer during your lunch hour," my mom said in a monotonous voice. "You haven't been here for lunch and obviously you haven't been spending your lunch hour volunteering. Jodee, what's going on? Daddy and I are worried."

I couldn't lie to my parents. The truth came spilling out. I described what happened between Jo Ellen and me, and how I was forced to make a horrible choice. I could barely get the words out because I was crying so hard. My dad walked over and scooped me up in his arms.

"Jodee, what you did was wrong," he admonished me gently. "You hurt Marianne and yourself because you allowed someone to make you smaller than you are. Jo Ellen was selfish and cruel, and you should have stood up to her. You knew what she was asking you to do was wrong, didn't you?" he asked firmly.

"Oh, yes, daddy," I replied. "I felt awful about it, but I didn't want to lose my best friend." I felt deeply ashamed of myself, yet also relieved that I didn't have to hide the truth anymore.

Later that day, my parents took me to Sister Clara's office. They explained that I had something important to tell her. I told Sister Clara everything that happened. She listened patiently.

"Oh, Sister, I'm so sorry," I cried. "Can I volunteer again, please?" I begged, afraid she would tell me to go away and never come back. Instead, she hugged me, then thanked my parents.

"I think there's a little girl who will be very happy to see you at lunch tomorrow," she said, smiling.

The next day, I returned to Sister Clara's classroom at lunchtime. When Marianne saw me, she ran up to me, grinning from ear to ear. "Marianne, I'm so sorry," I whispered. She grabbed my hand and pulled me toward the chalkboard, where she was drawing a picture of a flower. "It's very pretty," I said. She beamed at my praise, then wrapped her arms around me and squeezed. It was the first time I had felt good since that day I saw Jo Ellen in the hallway.

As the weeks passed, life seemed to be getting back to normal. Jo Ellen had even come around a bit. During recess one day, she started talking to me again. But I think she may have only been trying to be nice because she was getting pressure from her parents. My mom had called them and explained what happened between Jo Ellen and me. They were upset by their daughter's behavior and had encouraged her to play with me. "At least she doesn't hate me anymore," I reassured myself. What difference did it make if her parents had made that decision for her?

As the school year progressed, I spent less and less time with Jo Ellen. Gradually, we drifted apart. I missed having a best friend to share everything with, so I focused my love and energy on Marianne and the other kids in the deaf program. They found joy in places where healthy children would never have looked.

I spent most of my summer vacation that year in the country with my cousins. They were a few years older than me, but they went out of their way to include me in their games, telling me that they didn't mind if I tagged along because I was mature for my age. As August came to a close, I couldn't wait to get back to school. I had to find a new best friend, one who would embrace Marianne and the other children in her program.

Fifth grade started out with promise. I was invited to two slumber parties the first week! During recess, two of the most popular girls wanted me to play on their team for Tag, and Greg, the cutest boy in school, walked me to math class. "This is going to be the best year ever," I said to myself confidently. The most wonderful part was that no one was giving me a hard time anymore about volunteering my time at the program for the deaf. A couple of the girls in my homeroom even told me they thought it was good that I enjoyed doing it.

As Thanksgiving approached, I was having the time of my life. I had auditioned for a young people's theater group called The Pitt Players, and was cast as Dorothy in their big holiday production of *The Wizard of Oz*. All the kids at school would be attending the play, and I was so excited, I could hardly see straight. Every day was a new adventure. Everything seemed to be great, so no one could have predicted what was coming.

One afternoon, a group of my classmates began teasing some of the deaf kids. They were calling them horrible names, and mocking their handicap. "Retards, retards, we all hate the retards," they sang out.

"Please stop," I said, trying to reason with them. "They can't hear you anyway."

"Retards, retards, God even hates the retards," they continued.

"Stop it!" I shouted. "Leave them alone. They never did anything to hurt you."

It was no use. Jo Ellen was leading their cruel cheer, and I couldn't stop any of them. The harder I tried, the meaner they became. They looked at me as if I had betrayed them. How dare I defend the retards? their eyes said. The next thing I knew, Sister Clara was running toward us, ruler in hand, ready to punish the guilty. Jo Ellen and the others scattered down the hall. Several of the deaf children were whimpering by the door to their classroom, frightened and confused.

"What happened here?" Sister Clara asked, angry and visibly shaken. "Jodee, who started it?"

"I don't know, Sister," I said with my face down, trying to hide my shame.

"Miss Blanco, don't you try to fool me," she said in a stern tone I'd never heard from this gentle nun before. "I want to know who's responsible for inciting this cruelty and I know you witnessed it."

I didn't want to tattle on my classmates. But I couldn't stand lying to Sister Clara again. These sweet kids deserved better than this, and I had to do what was right this time.

"Jo Ellen and Greg," I confessed. "They started it."

"Thank you, Jodee. I know it was hard for you to be honest with me about this, but you did the honorable thing. I'm proud of you."

By the next day, it was all over school that I had ratted on Jo Ellen and Greg. The principal suspended them both for a week. No one would talk to me. I was in anguish. During recess, everyone ignored me. Later that afternoon, I found spoiled food from the garbage bin stuffed inside my bookbag.

At least I had the play to look forward to. I enjoyed rehearsals and got along well with the other kids in the theater group. "Things aren't so bad," I told myself. My dad said I showed strength of character. How many fifth graders could boast that? "Besides," I reassured myself, "everyone will see me in the play and forget this awful incident."

I was performing in the Sunday matinee. Dress rehearsal was Wednesday evening. On Friday morning, the local community paper printed a feature story about The Pitt Players' opening weekend. They ran a full-page photo of me in costume that they had taken during dress rehearsal. By the time mid-afternoon rolled around, everyone in school had seen the article. They were impressed by it. No one our age had ever been covered in the newspaper before. *Please, God, mom says things only happen if they're your will. Please let it be your will that the kids at school like me again.*

At the end of school that day, Terry, Jo Ellen's new best

friend and one of the most popular girls in our class, approached me.

"I saw you in the paper," she said. "Wow, what does it feel like?"

"It's okay, I guess," I replied, embarrassed and unsure of what to say.

"I'm having a slumber party on Saturday night and you're invited if you'd like to come," she offered.

Finally! I was back in the good graces of my peers. They had forgiven me! "Oh, yes, I'd love to come," I said, flooded with relief. I was so happy that I nearly floated home.

"Mom, you'll never guess what happened!" I screamed, barreling through the back door and flinging my bookbag onto the kitchen counter. "Terry invited me to her slumber party Saturday night," I said. "They don't hate me anymore. I'm so excited!"

"Angel, that's wonderful," mom responded. "I told you they'd come around. But honey, you can't go to that slumber party on Saturday night. You've got the play on Sunday afternoon. You've got to be at the theater by eight A.M. Jodee, you've worked so hard on this play. If you don't get a good night's sleep on Saturday, how will you be able to perform? You could end up letting yourself and the rest of The Pitt Players down," she explained.

"Mom, no, please let me go. If I tell Terry I'm not coming, I'll lose my chance of making friends with her and the other girls again," I said, fighting back tears. "You can't do this to me!"

"Jodee, you wanted to audition for *The Wizard of Oz*. It was your dream to be Dorothy. You have a responsibility and

I wouldn't be a good mom if I let you neglect it," she said. "Explain the circumstances to Terry. She'll understand."

"No, she won't. I won't be tired. I promise I won't stay up all night. Please let me go. Please!" I begged.

"No," she said firmly. "That's final."

That night, I cried and cried. It was all so unfair. Playing Dorothy was my dream, but school was still my reality. I was turning into the class outcast and Terry's party could be my salvation. Why couldn't my mom understand this? All she cared about was that I might be tired. What difference did it make? The play was one afternoon. School was every day.

The next morning, I told Terry I couldn't attend her slumber party. "Terry, my mom won't let me go because I have the play on Sunday," I tried to explain.

"You just don't want to come because you think you're better than me," she responded.

"No, that isn't true," I protested, feeling the promise of her friendship slipping away. "I don't care about this stupid play and I don't think I'm better than you."

"Yes, you do. You're nothing but a stuck-up actress. By the way, I only invited you because my mom told me to," Terry said. "Nobody wanted you there anyway." And with that, she turned on her heel and walked off. I was devastated.

On Sunday morning, I tried to push thoughts of the unpleasant scene with Terry into the back of my mind as I prepared for the show. I loved the activity backstage, the chaos in the dressing rooms as parents fussed with their children's costumes, the smell of the makeup, and the clanking of props and sets being hustled onto the stage. It was a world that had become my substitute for a social life.

Both my parents were backstage, giving me a pep talk. "Honey, break a leg," dad said encouragingly. "That's what professional actors always say before a performance."

"Jodee, remember to stand straight and project," my mom reminded me as she tightened my pigtails. The director, Mrs. Pitt, an energetic woman in her forties who had been gaining national celebrity for her work in children's theater, gently began escorting parents out of the dressing rooms.

"Mom, will any of the kids from school be in the audience?" I asked, without much hope.

"I wanted to surprise you, but I might as well tell you now," my mom said, her eyes twinkling. "I called some of the mothers. All your classmates will be here."

"Oh, mom, thank you!"

The show was a success. For two hours, I really was Dorothy. During the curtain call, when I took a bow, my dad came up on stage and handed me a vibrant bouquet of flowers. He was so handsome that day. Afterward, Terry, Jo Ellen, and several of the other kids from school came backstage to congratulate me. Though they were smiling and complimenting my performance, they seemed uncomfortable, as if they were being forced to eat a vegetable they didn't like. I pretended not to notice. I had just experienced my lifelong fantasy of playing Dorothy in *The Wizard of Oz*. But inside, I felt hollow.

In school on Monday morning, I thanked Jo Ellen and Terry for coming to the play. "It meant so much to me that you were there," I said, longing for their friendship again.

"It was fun," Terry said.

"Yeah," Jo Ellen chimed in.

"How did you memorize all those lines?" Terry asked.

"It wasn't that bad," I replied. "My mom practiced with me every day, and after a while, they just stayed in my head," I explained.

"See ya," Terry said.

"Yeah, see ya later," Jo Ellen said. *Maybe I can win them back. They're talking to me again.*

My optimism was short-lived. As fifth grade progressed, the social atmosphere at school began to shift in subtle but profound ways. Many of my classmates had started forming cliques. Being accepted by one of these groups was all that mattered. You were either in or out. If you weren't a cheerleader or an athlete, an honor student, or a member of the "tough" crowd, you might as well have been invisible.

I noticed other changes, too. Instead of being admired for participating in class the way we were in earlier grades, those of us who raised our hands frequently were now laughed at and labeled teacher's pets. Making fun of people, even if you didn't want to, was the new price of social acceptance by the group. The rules were simple. It was either shun or be shunned. The meaner you were to the "rejects," the more popular you became with the other members of your clique. If you weren't willing to go along with the crowd, *you* would become the "reject." Kids who had always been sweet and caring were becoming unkind in order to impress their friends.

"Why do you use such big words?" Eddie asked me one afternoon during recess. "You don't even know what they mean."

I liked learning new words, and would practice using them at school. No one had ever teased me about it before.

"I do too know what they mean," I responded.

"You're a liar and stuck up. Why don't you go to a different school? Nobody here likes you."

I had an enormous crush on Eddie. "Please don't say that," I replied, crestfallen, remembering him breaking the piñata at my ninth birthday party and the fun we had that day. Behind me, I heard the shuffle of gym shoes on the pavement. I turned around. Two of Eddie's buddies were walking toward us. "She's a freak," said one of them.

"Yeah, Eddie, why are you talking to the freak?" asked the other.

"I told her to go to another school because we all hate her here," Eddie retorted. "Freak, freak, nobody likes the freak," they sang mockingly. "Freak, freak, nobody likes the freak," they repeated over and over, a mantra of exclusion.

I ran across the school parking lot, their words echoing in my head like chimes. Winded and disoriented, with my chest burning for breath, I ducked into the drugstore and called my mom from a pay phone.

"Mom, please come get me. I can't go back there. Please," I begged.

"Jodee, where are you?" she asked, her voice thick with dread.

"I'm at Walgreens," I sobbed.

"I'll be there in five minutes."

Mom took me home, made me a grilled cheese sandwich, and put me into bed, where I slept until the next morning. When I came down for breakfast, my father told me that I had to return to school—I couldn't give Eddie or his friends the satisfaction of knowing they hurt me. "Ignore them and they'll stop bothering you," my parents said. They would never know how desperately wrong that advice was.

The children in the deaf program suffered the most. It wasn't only a few individuals who teased them now. Entire groups ganged up on them. They were an easy mark because they couldn't fight back. The handicapped weren't the only targets. Anyone who chose to be different was picked on. It was either conform or be cast out. I couldn't do it. I had made that mistake in the past when I turned my back on Marianne. I was determined not to be weak like that again.

By the end of the fifth grade, I was bereft. My outlook might have been different if loneliness was familiar; if I had never known popularity. But from first grade until fourth, everyone liked me. To go from being admired to becoming the school outcast was too much of a shock.

My parents were conflicted about what to do. They couldn't stand seeing me come home from school every day in tears, but they were also worried that if they let me transfer schools, they'd be advocating escape, and setting an example that it was okay to run away from problems. They were caught between wanting to save me from pain and wanting to teach me how to transcend it. They decided to let me enjoy the summer, and that we would make a decision in the fall. I was still active with The Pitt Players. Thank God for that theater group.

In September, I told my parents that I wanted to return to Holy Ascension; that I didn't want to run away, I wanted to be strong. They agreed. Sixth grade started out okay. The teasing was minimal. I toned down my vocabulary and refrained from raising my hand in class. If the teacher called on me, fine. If not, even better. I literally sat on my hands sometimes to remind myself that I didn't want to be the teacher's pet. My efforts seemed to be paying off. During recess, my classmates started inviting me to play Four Square and Red Rover with them again. I wasn't popular, but at least I wasn't getting picked on incessantly. "I have to remain hopeful and keep up the good work," I told myself.

Though I was encouraged, I was still lonely. Not being teased is one thing. Not having friends is another. "Please God," I begged, "Make the kids at school like me again."

It happened Halloween night. My classmates rang my doorbell and asked if I wanted to go trick-or-treating with them. I was so excited and relieved I almost cried. They were giving me another chance. I grabbed my bright orange plastic pumpkin bag and ran out the door, thinking that maybe God had heard my prayers. There was only one catch: They wanted me to join them in playing a nasty joke on an elderly woman who lived up the street. They were going to pelt her house with raw eggs and toilet paper, and were enlisting my help as an accomplice.

"She's a weird old biddy," Jo Ellen hissed.

"Let's make her tear her hair out," Terry shouted.

"Can you see her in her stupid robe cleaning up this

mess!" Greg cried, bursting out laughing.

I refused to join in because I felt so bad for this lady. I told them what they wanted to do was mean and horrible. In an instant, the focus of their disdain switched from the old woman to *me*. The comeback I had longed for was a bust.

The next day, my parents met with Sister Jeannine, the school principal. "I don't understand what all the fuss is about," she said after my mom and dad shared some of my experiences at school. "She should make more of an effort to blend in. Kids will be kids. You have to let them fight their own battles. If she's not willing to try harder to get along with the other children, perhaps it's best if she transfers to another school," Sister concluded tersely.

The next month, I was enrolled at Morgan Hills Academy, a private school for the "intellectually and artistically gifted."

chapter four

Darkening

Skies

"It's all set," mom said cheerfully. "You'll start at Morgan Hills Academy in one week."

"Mom, I'm not sure I want to go to this school," I admitted. "There are people *buried* on campus. I saw their tombstones in the back garden during orientation! It was gross."

"Jodee, those aren't graves," my mom explained. "Those are memorials for students who died in one of the world wars."

"Mom, it's not a military school, for God's sake. Those memorials are creepy. And did you notice how old and depressing the building is?" I asked, horrified at the thought of walking through dark, dingy halls every day.

"Honey, Morgan Hills is one of the finest private schools in this part of the country," she pointed out encouragingly. "The building is a landmark. You always talk about where you might go to college. Many of the best universities are in old buildings."

"I guess you're right," I replied, forcing a smile. "Do you think the kids will like me at this new school?"

"Of course they will," my mom said. "The students at Morgan Hills are serious about their studies. They won't tease you for participating in class or using big words. You'll finally be someplace where you have something in common with the other children your age."

"I'm still nervous," I said, wishing I didn't have to face any of this.

"Everything will be wonderful," she reassured me. "I have a good feeling."

As the first day of school approached, I grew optimistic. This could be my new beginning. I wouldn't have to wear a school uniform anymore, which was a relief. I couldn't stand the plaid skirt and starched white shirt we had to wear at Catholic school. And classes were smaller. There were only thirty students in the sixth grade at Morgan Hills Academy, fifteen to a classroom. At Holy Ascension, there had been thirty students per classroom. The subjects also promised to be more interesting. Sixth graders could study ancient history, literature, French, astronomy, and even paleontology, none of which were taught at Holy Ascension. I was especially looking forward to ancient history and pale-ontology. I adored learning about archaeological ruins and fossils.

Though I was going to be the only new girl at school, I did know Callie, one of my new classmates. Since we were both members of The Pitt Players, she and I had been in numerous plays together. She promised to introduce me to everyone the first day of school. "You'll love the academy," she said, full of enthusiasm. "The teachers are really cool and I've told all my friends about you."

"Callie, I'm scared that I won't fit in," I confessed. "You and your friends have known each other since the first grade. I'm going to feel like an outsider."

"Jodee, the kids at this school are really nice. You'll see. Trust me."

I sure hoped she was right. If my classmates didn't like me at this new school, I was sunk. My parents would stop believing in me. I'd heard them talking the night before, when they thought I was asleep.

"We've got to be honest with ourselves," my father had said. "We can't always let Jodee run away from her problems. If she doesn't get along at Morgan Hills, there may be something wrong with her."

"What are you saying?" my mom asked.

"I'm saying that we should take our daughter to a psychiatrist, someone who could figure out what's wrong," he explained, calmly.

"It isn't Jodee's fault," my mom argued, raising her voice. "She's a leader, not a follower, and she's the class scapegoat because of it."

"I don't care what the reasons are," dad retorted. "The kid has been crying herself to sleep for a year. I can't stand seeing her hurt, and if she's bringing this on herself, if she's doing something to cause rejection, we've got to get to the bottom of it."

"I'm surprised you're aware she's been so miserable. You're barely ever home," mom said.

"Let's not get into that," dad responded tightly. "I want you to call the pediatrician and ask him to recommend a good child psychiatrist. I don't care what it costs or how far we have to travel. I want to know why our daughter is a misfit."

Hearing those words from my dad hit me hard. Is that

how he saw me—as a *misfit*? Anger swelled inside me. I felt sick to my stomach.

"I'll get the name of the best specialist in Chicago," mom said. "But let's wait a few months and see what happens with the new school before we make an appointment."

"All right," dad acquiesced. "We'll give it until Christmas vacation."

That night, crouched in the darkness, eavesdropping on my parents' discussion, I felt truly alone for the first time in my life. The only two people in the world who had been on my side through this whole mess no longer believed in me.

Words that had once comforted me flooded my memory, making the conversation I was overhearing hurt even more . . .

Your classmates don't hate you. You're just ahead of your years. They'll catch up to you, and you'll be successful and have more friends than you could possibly imagine. One day, just like in The Ugly Duckling, *you, too, will become a swan.* ∎

What happened? How could my parents have had such a change of heart? Maybe dad was right and there *was* something wrong with me. Maybe it really was my fault that I didn't fit in.

What little self-confidence I had vanished that night. My parents were contemplating taking me to a psychiatrist. I was nervous enough about adjusting to a new school, let alone knowing that if I blew it, I'd be dragged to a shrink's office.

"Angel, time to get up," mom said brightly as she walked into my room and switched on the lights. "It's your first day, aren't you excited?"

"Yeah, but I'm scared, too," I replied.

"Jodee, this is a new beginning. Just be yourself," she said. "Hurry up and get dressed so you have time to eat a good breakfast before the school bus comes."

"Okay, mom," I answered.

After forcing down a few mouthfuls of scrambled eggs, I put on my jacket and hugged my mom goodbye. As she held me, I snuggled into her embrace, not wanting to leave. She gently pulled away and handed my bookbag to me. Then, cupping my face in her hands, she looked into my eyes and told me that she would always be there for me, and that no matter what, she and daddy loved me with all their hearts.

"There's the bus," she said. "Go on now."

The bus driver, a robust older woman in her sixties, welcomed me warmly. "You must be Jodee Blanco, the new sixth grader," she said, smiling.

"Yes," I responded self-consciously.

"I'm Mrs. Andrews. This is bus number twenty-six. I'll be taking you home after school, too," she explained. "Why don't you sit in the third row on the left, next to Debbie. You girls are in the same class. Debbie, please introduce Jodee to the rest of the students on the bus."

"Hi," Debbie said cheerfully, as I settled in next to her. Petite, with sparkling blue eyes and long blond hair, Debbie reminded me of a young Farrah Fawcett. I liked her immediately. "Callie has told us all about you. Everyone wants to meet you," she exclaimed.

I was overjoyed. The tension inside me began to subside. I felt lighter, as if hope itself had lifted me out of a dark hole. "Morgan Hills Academy will be okay," I said to myself. For the rest of the ride, Debbie introduced me to the other students on the bus. Ranging from first through eighth grade, they were friendly and curious, asking me questions about my old school and my favorite subjects.

"Callie, wait up," I heard Debbie shout out the bus window as we pulled into the school parking lot. Callie, clad in a red-and-white cheerleading uniform, turned around, smiling and waving.

"Jodee, welcome to Morgan Hills," she said, bursting with enthusiasm.

"Thanks! I'm so excited," I replied. "By the way, you never told me you were a cheerleader. At my old school, you weren't even allowed to try out until the seventh grade."

"Yeah, I made the squad over the summer," she replied proudly. "Come on, Debbie and I will show you where your locker is. Then you can meet everyone."

As Callie, Debbie, and I walked across campus toward the main building, I asked them about Mr. Warren and Ms. Gorge, the sixth grade teachers. "Mr. Warren's sweet. He gives a lot of pop quizzes, but as long as you pay attention in class and do the reading assignments, you can pretty much get a good grade. He's also a real babe," Debbie confided, blushing.

"Yeah, but what about old lady Gorge?" Callie chimed in, rolling her eyes at Debbie. "Don't tell anyone we told you," she whispered, "but I overheard my mom say that Ms. Gorge used to be an alcoholic, and that's why her hands shake sometimes. And she's ancient, sixty years old at least. She can be such a bitch and she's *really* moody."

I was thrilled to be included in such top-secret girl talk.

"Don't forget that perfume of hers," Debbie added. "She wears L' Air du Temps, and it stinks up the whole classroom. Yuck."

"We better hurry," Callie urged. "I want you to meet everyone before class starts."

"Okay," I said. I was finally fitting in and it was heaven.

"Last one to reach the main building is a rotten egg," Debbie yelled. Racing across the schoolyard—the early September chill pinching our cheeks, the autumn leaves crunching beneath our shoes—I felt free and exhilarated.

"You win, Callie," Debbie and I shouted in unison, catching our breath. Our sides ached from laughing so hard. Callie and Debbie were two of the most popular girls in the sixth grade. Having them introduce me to the rest of the class would ensure my acceptance.

Morgan Hills Academy resembled an English school for boys. The gymnasium was located at the far end of the property, behind the school gardens. The cafeteria, an imposing stone structure with cathedral ceilings and stained glass windows, stood in the middle of the grounds. The North Wing, where the sixth grade was located, was the largest of the school's three buildings. Though it had been renovated numerous times throughout the decades, there was a residual grayness about it, as if years of decay were still present beneath its fresh veneer.

The inside of the North Wing was sparse and utilitarian. The hallways were slate blue, lined with rows of navy-colored lockers. The classrooms were painted bright white. The effect made me uneasy, as if I were walking through the corridors of a hospital, not a school.

A group of students were chatting near the lockers outside Mr. Warren's room. When they saw me approaching with Debbie and Callie, they hurried toward us. Eager and curious, they began asking me questions. "Are you the new student? Where did you transfer from? Are you trying out for any sports? Where do you live? Do you want to sit with us at lunch?" I was surrounded by my new classmates. One after another, they introduced themselves. I couldn't keep their names straight. It was dizzying.

"Hi, I'm Peter," said a cute boy with light brown hair, and warm, friendly green eyes. "You'll love our school. It's really cool here."

"It's good to meet you," I responded, forming an instant crush on him.

"I'm Steve. Callie says you like drama. The sixth grade class is doing *Tom Sawyer* this year. You should try out," the boy standing next to Peter volunteered.

"I like doing plays," I replied, excited.

"Jodee, I'd like you to meet some more of my friends," Callie interrupted, letting me know by the tone of her voice that now I was meeting the in-crowd.

"Hi," I said, reminding myself to swallow and to blink. I desperately needed their acceptance.

Shooting a knowing glance in Callie's direction, Kat, a statuesque girl with long black hair and deep-set brown eyes, stepped forward to introduce herself. Kat had an air of authority about her, as if she knew exactly who she was and what she wanted out of life. *Whatever you do, don't let her see that you're intimidated.*

"It's nice to meet you," I said, trying to look as confident as I could.

"Welcome to Morgan Hills. Where did you transfer from?" she asked, her face as expressionless as cement.

"Holy Ascension," I answered.

"Ugh, Catholic school. Didn't you hate it? I hear the nuns can be pretty mean," she said, watching my body language and deciding whether or not she was going to like me.

"They were okay," I said, a sudden image of Sister Rose and the security she represented giving me a pang. "I think I'll like it here better."

"Why don't you sit next to Jackie and me first period?" Kat offered, her demeanor softening. "There's an empty desk between us. I'm sure Mr. Warren won't mind."

My confidence surged. If Kat was warming up to me, I knew I had made it over the first hurdle. "That'd be terrific," I said gratefully.

By the time the bell rang for first period, I had met almost everyone in the sixth grade. As I settled into my seat, someone tapped me hard on the shoulder. I turned around to see who it was. Standing directly behind my desk was a tall girl with stringy blond hair and horn-rimmed glasses.

"I'm Dara," she announced haughtily.

"Hi," I responded, immediately sensing Dara was someone you would never want to be your enemy. "I'm Jodee Blanco, the new student."

"Obviously," she retorted tersely, studying my reaction.

"Yeah, it's really obvious, isn't it?" I agreed, my mind racing to come up with something smart and funny to say next that would impress her. "I stick out like a bra on a bulldog," I quipped, pleased with my quick wit.

The entire class overheard my remark and burst out laughing. Before Dara could respond, Mr. Warren entered the room, and walked over to me. "I see you're having no problem getting acquainted with everyone," he grinned. "You must be Jodee Blanco. Welcome to sixth grade homeroom."

"Thank you, Mr. Warren," I said.

When Mr. Warren began roll call, Dara slipped me a note under the desk. I unfolded the small piece of spiral notebook paper. It read:

You're really cool.

Overcome with delight, I stuffed the note inside my bookbag, anxious to show my parents the proof that I was no longer a misfit.

My first few months at Morgan Hills Academy passed swiftly and without incident. I was keeping up my grades and getting along well with all my classmates. Even Kat and Dara had accepted me as one of the gang. I had formed a bond with Callie and Debbie. We were inseparable. We gossiped and shared secrets, experimented with makeup, slept over at each other's houses on weekends, and talked for hours on the phone about our favorite subject: boys. Callie and I both had a crush on Peter. Debbie liked Steve.

Many of the sixth graders were already starting to go

steady. Parents and teachers suspected it, but they weren't concerned because in their minds, how much trouble could twelve-year-olds get into when they couldn't drive or go on dates alone? The most that could happen, they thought, would be an innocent kiss in the schoolyard. Their naïveté would cost all of us dearly.

Christmas was approaching and Callie's mom had agreed to let her host an evening holiday party with boys and girls. Callie was thrilled. She, Debbie, and I spent hours doing the invitations. As I was licking the envelopes, I noticed that a name was missing and asked Callie about it.

"All the invitations are there," she said.

"What about Dave?" I asked. Shy and awkward, Dave was a loner. He wasn't ridiculed by his classmates; he was ignored. Earlier in the week, he had overheard Debbie and me talking about the party. Later on the way to gym, he pulled me aside. "Do you think I'll get invited?" he asked. It had probably taken him all day just to muster up the courage to approach me. "Of course you'll be invited," I had answered.

"You're totally joking, right?" Callie asked, jolting me back to the present. "He's nobody."

"Yeah, but his feelings could really be hurt," I replied.

"Callie, maybe Jodee's right . . . " Before Debbie could finish her sentence, Callie silenced her with a withering stare. I felt bad. But I was afraid if I pushed the issue, it would diminish Callie's opinion of me. It was too great a risk. Dave would have to live with disappointment. I wasn't going to be the outcast again.

I quickly switched the subject to what we would be wearing to the party. As Debbie and Callie blathered on about their party outfits, guilt turned my stomach. I had just done to someone else what had been done to me so often in the past. It was like the incident with Jo Ellen and Marianne all over again. But it was easier this time. Dave was a typical, healthy kid. At least he could protect himself. Maybe finding out who you were and going separate ways is just part of growing up. But part of me knew it was more than that, something I couldn't explain away so easily.

When I was the outcast, I never thought about the other kids who were also getting rejected. I couldn't see past my own pain. It never occurred to me that one day, I would be the source of such pain. I was beginning to realize that it was all part of a cycle of social survival. Some poor kid like Dave would always be the class scapegoat. I had to stop trying to be the hero. "It's Callie's party," I told myself firmly. "If she doesn't want Dave there, that isn't my fault."

By the end of the week, the invitations to the party had been delivered. "It's only Thursday," Dave said in between classes. "Maybe my invitation will come today in the mail."

I looked down, too ashamed to answer.

"I wasn't invited, was I?" he concluded.

"No, Dave," I said.

"That's okay. I didn't think I would be anyhow," he said sadly. Slinging his bookbag over his shoulder, he walked off to class. *Stop feeling so guilty. He'll get over it. Years from now, he probably won't even remember any of this.* I would never know how wrong I was.

As Saturday night loomed closer, rather than feeling excitement about Callie's party, I began to experience a nagging sense of foreboding.

"Angel, what's wrong?" my mom asked, concerned, as I was dressing for the party.

"Nothing, I'm fine."

I had been telling my parents that everything at school was wonderful. I didn't want to risk them finding out that even though I was making friends, I was starting to have doubts about whether or not it was worth it. At least when I was a social failure, I had a clear conscience. "But anything is better," I thought, "than seeing a psychiatrist." My dad wouldn't care about the details this time around. If he got a mere inkling that something was askew, I would be whisked to the shrink's office, no questions asked.

As we pulled into Callie's driveway, half of me wanted to turn around and go home. The other half of me couldn't wait to experience my first boy-girl evening party. Callie's mother, lithe and beautifully dressed in cream-colored slacks and a matching blouse, greeted me at the door. "Jodee, you know your way around. The party's upstairs," she said, waving to my mom.

Callie lived in a large, two-story Georgian in one of Chicago's oldest and most affluent neighborhoods. When Callie's parents bought the house, they renovated the attic, transforming it into a recreation room for the kids. As I climbed the stairs, I could hear rock music pounding from above, and the sounds of muffled laughter. I wondered if Peter had arrived yet. Just thinking about him gave me goosebumps.

When I reached the top of the stairs, the attic door was locked. I banged on it loudly. Finally, the door opened. "Hey, you guys, Jodee's here!" Callie shouted to everyone inside, trying to make herself heard over Elton John's "Island Girl," which blared out of the stereo speakers.

"Callie, why did you lock the door?" I asked.

"Because we're playing Spin the Bottle and I don't want my mom walking in on us," she explained matter of factly.

"What's the big deal about Spin the Bottle?" I replied, confused. "It's just Truth or Dare. You either choose to answer a question or take on a dare. We play it all the time. Your mom doesn't care."

"No silly, we're not playing Truth or Dare Spin the Bottle, we're playing Strip Spin the Bottle," she said, lowering her voice to a whisper.

"What do you mean, *strip*?"

"You know, when the bottle points to you, you have to take off a piece of your clothing. The last person with any clothes on wins. Jewelry doesn't count. Come on, it's fun," she said, locking the door behind us.

"What's the worst that could happen?" I reassured myself. I joined the game. Besides, Peter was there, and I wanted to impress him with how cool I could be. Everyone was sitting cross-legged in a circle. There were eight girls and seven boys. It didn't take long before the floor was strewn with sweaters, scarves, and other garments. Soon, I was down to my jeans and blouse. Debbie, who was well developed for her age, was by now clad in nothing but her underwear. The boys were staring at her body. It made me uncomfortable. With every spin of the Coke bottle, my muscles tensed.

"Jodee, take something off," Callie sang cheerfully as the nose of the bottle stopped directly in front of my left knee.

"Okay," I replied with feigned nonchalance. Slowly, I unbuttoned my blouse and dropped it beside me. Debbie and I looked at each other. I could tell that she was just as nervous as I was. The hollow humming sound of the bottle as it spun on the carpeting seemed to grow louder. It pointed to Debbie again.

"Come on Debbie, take it off," chanted the boys. I felt so sorry for her. She was near tears, but didn't want anyone thinking she was a sissy. As her cheeks turned beet-red, she yanked off her training bra. Everyone giggled except Peter. He saw the expression on Debbie's face.

"Yeah, Debbie! It's your turn to spin," Callie commanded.

"No," Peter remarked. "This is getting boring. Let's do something else," he declared, saving Debbie from further humiliation. Peter was the most popular boy at school—what he said went. His buddies quickly echoed their agreement.

"Yeah, let's play Kiss or Tell," Steve suggested.

"What's that?" I asked.

"It's easy," he replied. "It's just like Truth or Dare except instead of doing a dare, you have to kiss who you're told to," he explained. "And it can't be a sissy kiss, it has to be a real kiss, you know, on the mouth with your tongue and everything."

"It's a blast," said Kat, hastily struggling back into her cardigan.

It occurred to me how much more precocious these kids were than my former classmates at Holy Ascension. I hadn't yet gotten my first kiss, and at twelve years old, they were already into necking and God knows what else. Catholic school was a sheltered environment compared to where I was now. *Act cool. You're finally part of the popular clique. Don't blow it by being a prude.*

We played the game. The bottle chose me twice. I got to kiss Steve, which I liked, and Peter, which made me realize how much more fun it is to kiss someone you're attracted to. But this kissing game wasn't enough for some of the kids who were familiar with more advanced sex play.

I could sense the atmosphere in the room begin to shift as some started to pair off into couples. The lights were turned off and candles lit. I sat there, stunned, half of me wanting to run, the other half wishing I could muster up the nerve to join in. Before I knew it, one of the couples snuck into the walk-in closet and closed the door. Unable to look away, I could see through the slats what was going on. I was horrified.

I ran downstairs to telephone my mom. "Mom, please pick me up," I cried.

"Angel, what is it, what's the matter?" she asked.

"Mom, what one couple is doing in the closet—it will make me turn red if I even have to talk about it," I sobbed.

"Where's Callie's mother?" my mom asked.

"She's in the kitchen getting the cake ready, I think. I'm on the phone in the den. Please don't say anything to her. I don't want to tell on Callie. Please, Callie will hate me. Can't you just pick me up and we'll tell Callie's mom that I have a stomachache?"

"Jodee, put Callie's mom on the phone now," she demanded.

"No, mom! Please," I pleaded.

"Now, Jodee."

I was crying hard. Callie's mom came rushing into the

kitchen. I handed her the phone.

"Oh, my God," she muttered, dropping the receiver and bolting up the stairs.

She caught everyone in the act. Shocked and furious, she screamed at Callie in front of everyone. It was awful. Then, she immediately began calling the other parents to tell them what had happened. By the time my mom arrived, Callie's mom had marched everyone down to the living room, where they were waiting—in dead silence—for their parents to pick them up.

"Oh, Joy, I'm so sorry about all this," she said. "I should never have left them unchaperoned."

"I don't blame you," my mom replied. "I wouldn't have thought something like this could happen at a party for twelve-year-olds either."

"You have a remarkable daughter. I'm grateful she had the common sense to call you," she added.

I winced at her words. I had just betrayed my best friend and the most popular kids at school. As mom and I were walking out, I turned and looked at Callie. Her eyes were cauldrons of rage. As I closed the door behind me, I was gripped by that old familiar fear.

When I arrived at school on Monday morning, the atmosphere was tense. Kat and Jackie ignored me at the lockers. Dara wouldn't speak to me. Callie avoided me. When the bell rang and everyone ran to first period home-room, I went into the hall, not wanting to face the rest of the day. Debbie saw me standing there and came up to me and put her arm around me.

"Jodee, all this will blow over," she said, trying to comfort me. "Honest, it will. Callie's angry now, but she'll get over it."

I was so grateful to Debbie for talking to me. She was taking a chance being my friend.

"Debbie, just how far did you go with Steve Saturday night at Callie's party?" I asked, unsure I could handle the truth.

"Not far. We were kissing and he tried to touch my breasts. That's when Callie's mom came running up the stairs, shouting. That's why I wanted to talk to you alone this morning before class. You saved my ass, literally," she confessed with a nervous chuckle. "I don't know what I would have done if a grown-up hadn't come running into the room. I like to think I would have stopped Steve, but there's a part of me that's afraid of being called a chicken."

"Then I'm glad I called my mom," I said.

"Yeah, me too," she said. "And don't worry about everybody else. I'm your friend and I'll always be your friend. Are you coming to class?"

"Yeah, I'll be there in a second. Just tell Mr. Warren that I went to the bathroom."

It had snowed that morning and I had worn my boots to school. I was so distracted that I had forgotten to change into my shoes. On the way to my locker, I stopped at the ladies room. Out of habit, I stepped inside the first stall to the right. When I looked down, floating in the toilet in a pool of urine was one of my favorite suede shoes. There was a note tied to the buckle with a piece of macramé string from art class. Repulsed, I lowered my hand into the water, and slowly extracted my ruined shoe out of the bowl. I turned over the note. Scrawled in indelible ink were the words:

Bitch, this is just the beginning.

My insides went numb. This was worse than I expected. Debbie was wrong. Nobody was going to forgive and forget what happened at Callie's party. They didn't understand why I did what I did. Hell, I wasn't sure I understood it myself.

Gathering my resolve, I threw my shoe in the garbage can, grabbed my bookbag, and made my way to Mr. Warren's class. The minute I walked into the room, I could feel the anger of my classmates. They had included me in their secrets. They had made me one of them. And I had betrayed those gifts. I was the enemy now. "At least Debbie is my friend," I consoled myself. Mom always told me if you have one good friend, that's everything. Right now I hoped she was right.

At lunchtime, no one would sit with me. I wasn't surprised, but it didn't make it hurt any less. As I was leaving the cafeteria, Dave stopped me. "I heard what happened," he remarked. "I know you wanted to invite me to Callie's party, but she wouldn't let you."

"Yes, that's right," I acknowledged.

"I don't want to hurt your feelings, but I can't talk to you anymore. Everyone gives me a hard enough time as it is. If Steve or any of his friends see me being friendly to you, things will get worse. I just wanted you to know it's not because I hate you, it's just that I don't have a choice."

I was touched. "Thanks for telling me. Don't worry, I understand."

No one talked to me on the bus ride home. The phone didn't ring that night. I was back in that lonely place. Debbie was trying to be supportive but I wondered how long she could keep it up. Eventually Callie and the others would force her to make a choice. I couldn't expect her to sacrifice friends she'd known since she was six years old just for me. What happened Saturday was my fault. She shouldn't have to pay for that.

As difficult as school was, coming home was harder. I couldn't let my parents know something was wrong because I was terrified they'd make me see the psychiatrist. It was like having a loaded gun aimed at my head. One wrong move, and *boom*.

Mom was waiting for me in the kitchen when I got home. "How did your day go, honey?" she asked anxiously.

"It was okay. Some of the kids are still mad at me, but I think this whole incident will be forgotten by Christmas," I said, avoiding her eyes.

"Angel, didn't I tell you everything would be all right?" said my mom. "You just have to have faith."

"Yeah, mom. I've got a bunch of homework. I'm going up to my room."

I had convinced her.

Every day, it was the same routine. The kids either ignored me or taunted me, snickering behind my back. Thank God I had Debbie. Her friendship sustained me. Some of the kids were starting to give her a hard time because of it, and I felt guilty about that.

"It's so great that you're my friend, but I don't think it's fair that you should have to pay for my mistakes," I said to Debbie on the bus ride home one day. "You don't have to be nice to me at school. We can still visit each other's houses, but when we're at school, you can pretend you don't like me anymore either. I know you're my friend, but it's not going to make me feel any better if everyone rejects you, too." I could see the relief on her face.

"Oh, Jodee," she said, gratefully. "I didn't want to say anything, but Callie and Dara have really been pressuring me. It'll be our secret that you're my best friend."

"Absolutely, Debbie. Our secret."

Pretending that Debbie didn't like me anymore when we were at school was tough on both of us. I actually think it was harder for Debbie because she felt guilty and was concerned that she was hurting me. I loved her for that.

As the weeks passed, my classmates found every opportunity they could to pick fights with me. Many of them had been punished severely by their parents for their behavior at Callie's party, and they blamed me for it.

Kat and Dara started to become physically abusive. Kat would bump into me in the halls, shoving me into the lockers. Dara would kick me in the legs and shins. One afternoon in the lavatory, she tried to burn the inside of my wrist with a lit cigarette. I attempted to scream, but Jackie clamped her hand across my mouth, and told me if I made a sound, she and Dara would beat me until I bled.

My parents had told me that the best way to handle bullies was to humiliate them with a brilliant and biting remark, then just turn and leave. "Don't give them the satisfaction of

knowing that they got to you," my mom and dad had counseled me countless times. "Ignore them and they'll stop bothering you."

So that's what I tried to do. Every time Dara, Kat, or
any of their friends abused me, instead of fighting back and
sticking up for my rights, I responded with a verbal comeback, or I acted as if they weren't there. The more I showed
how "mature" I could be, the more determined they were to
get my goat. What had started out as simple payback for
being a tattletale had mutated into something far more
serious.

Peter was my hero. "Why don't you leave Jodee alone?"
he asked Dara one morning before class. "I know everybody's
mad at her, but that doesn't mean it's okay to beat on her."

"Peter, don't tell me that you're siding with that prissy
rat," Dara said.

"No, Dara, it's just that I don't think it's right to hit her.
Besides, if Mr. Warren or Ms. Gorge caught you, you could
get into real trouble."

"Screw you," she spat as she walked away.

"Thanks, Peter," I said, overhearing their row.

"That's okay," he smiled.

My heart soared. Peter still liked me. He was my protector. I wasn't alone, after all. I could endure the rest of the
year. I clung to that knowledge that even if nobody else
would be my friend, at least Peter and Debbie cared about
me. That night, when my parents inquired how I was doing
at school, I told them things were okay. For the first time in
weeks, it was the truth.

Christmas break came and went quickly. Maybe by now,

everyone would have forgotten about Callie's party. I had talked to Peter and Debbie the night before our first day back, and they told me we were still friends. When I got to Mr. Warren's class, Kat and Dara looked right past me. It was no use. I couldn't win them back. That afternoon, following gym class, Dara, Kat, and a few other girls approached me in the locker room. "Where's your pretty new sweater?" they asked.

"What are you talking about?" I replied. "It's in my locker. Why?"

"Are you sure?" they asked, snickering.

I opened my locker and, sure enough, the brand-new white sweater that my Aunt Evie had given me for Christmas was missing. "What did you do with it?" I asked.

"Screw you," they retorted, running out of the locker room giggling.

I searched everywhere for my sweater. Finally, I found it scrunched up into a ball under the radiator near the janitor's closet, with several open cans of Coke lying on top of it, the sugary liquid forming great brown splotches on the angora. Carefully picking the sticky, wet garment up off the floor, I folded it neatly and placed it inside my gym bag. With any luck, I could use some Woolite to remove the stains.

With nothing else to wear for the rest of the day, I then put my gym shirt back on, threw on my jacket, grabbed my books, and left for English class. As I closed the front door of the gym, Steve approached me, smiling, and asked if he could walk me to class.

"Wow, that would be great," I replied, thrilled but confused by the unexpected request. He had been giving me the cold shoulder since Callie's party.

"Jodee, I'm not mad anymore," he confirmed. Then, he extended his hand. I thought it was peculiar. He'd never tried to hold my hand before, but I was excited that he was being nice to me again. When I reached out to take his hand, he gripped my wrist and started twisting it until my knees began to buckle. Then, Kat, Dara, Jackie, and several other students came at me from behind. They grabbed my hands and feet and dragged me across the parking lot behind the main campus, chanting "We're going to kill you." They started kicking me and spitting on me. They ripped open my bookbag and threw the contents all over the ground. Oddly, I wasn't frightened. Being killed held the promise of relief.

Lying on the pavement, curled up in a ball, listening to them laugh at me, all I could think of was how I was going to explain what happened to me when I arrived home. My jacket and pants were ripped and filthy. My hair was full of gravel and spit. My arms were scratched and bruised.

I remained there in the fetal position, rocking back and forth until the bell rang and I heard my tormentors leave. I sat up and opened my eyes. I gathered my books and papers and slowly stood up. I was in terrible pain. Not knowing what else to do, I went to the nurses' office.

"I was running to class and fell," I fibbed. "I ruined my sweater, so I put my gym shirt back on." The nurse, a persnickety woman, stared at me, disbelief written all across her face.

"Could you help me clean up?" I asked, wincing. "These cuts really hurt."

"Jodee, you're not telling the truth," she observed, sternly.

"Please, I can't be a tattletale again. Let me handle this my own way," I begged.

"All right, but if I see you in this state again, I'm contacting your parents," she said.

"Fair enough."

Though she did as much as she could for me, the signs of the attack were still visible. "Are you all right?" Ms. Gorge inquired as I eased myself carefully into my desk.

Every eye in the room was on me. If I said anything to Ms. Gorge, I'd be digging my own grave.

"I tripped and fell."

"Do you want to go home?" she asked.

"No, I'm okay."

When Peter and Debbie found out what had happened to me after gym, they were shocked. "Jodee, why didn't you yell for help?" Peter asked. "I was helping coach MacMillan set up for football practice. If I'd heard you, I'd have kicked Steve right in the teeth."

"Yeah," Debbie interrupted. "Screw pretending that I'm not your friend. We'd both have tried to stop them."

"I know you guys would have," I said gratefully. "I was so confused I couldn't think."

The beating in the school parking lot was the first of many such incidents. I wished that my parents and the other adults would have counseled me differently about how to handle being picked on. My family had always treated me like a miniature adult, and that's how I interacted with my peers. I longed to beat the daylights out of Dara. When I lay in bed at night, I fantasized about slapping Kat across her face, punching Steve in the stomach, and throwing Jackie's new leather purse in the mud. Rage was building inside me. But instead of allowing myself the blessed release of giving my classmates what they deserved, and maybe winning back their respect in the process, I rose above it and turned the other cheek.

The kids at school misinterpreted my behavior. They thought I was being stuck-up and condescending. It turned their resentment for what I had done one Saturday night into disdain for who I was as a person. Even Peter and Debbie eventually distanced themselves from me, unable to bear the ridicule and rejection. Though they never actively engaged in any teasing or abuse, their fellow students had pressured them into disassociating themselves from me.

I dreaded my parents finding out that I was a social failure again, so every afternoon when I got back from school, I carefully hid any evidence of abuse. I applied makeup to my arms and legs so my mom couldn't see the bruises where I'd been punched or kicked. I soaked the bloodstains and mud off my clothes in the tub before she got home. If I had to cry, I turned the stereo on so no one could hear me. When anyone asked how school was going, I said that everything was terrific and that I'd never been happier.

Mr. Warren and Ms. Gorge had to know something was wrong, but they never said or did anything. One afternoon, Steve and Dara followed me to the school bus.

"What's wrong?" Dara hissed. "Are you afraid?"

"Why should you be afraid of us?" Steve cooed ominously. "We're your friends."

I thought I might throw up. "Come on, you guys. Just leave me alone." They both burst into laughter. Now, I didn't care what happened to me. I was seething with rage.

"Go to hell, you bastard," I cried. Then Steve hit me in the chest so hard that it knocked the wind clean out of me. Struggling to catch my breath, I fell to the ground and sobbed. Mr. Warren saw me as he was getting into his car, and came over.

"What happened?" he asked.

"Steve hit me. I want you give him a detention," I demanded. "I want him to get in trouble."

"Jodee, I could give him a detention. What he did was wrong. But don't you think it would be better if you and Steve worked out your problem between the two of you without school intervention? If I give him a detention, you're only going to be labeled a tattletale. In the real world, we must learn to fight our own battles," Mr. Warren said patronizingly.

Now I felt more alone than ever. "I guess you're right."

That night, my situation became clear to me. I had nowhere to turn. If I went to my teachers, my classmates would get into trouble, and it would make things worse. I couldn't go to my parents for help because they would drag me to the psychiatrist's office. It was bad enough that I was being treated like a freak by my peers. I sure didn't want a shrink labeling me as one. On top of that, I was frequently absent. I had chronic strep throat and constant stomachaches. In a way, I was glad. It meant that I didn't have to face school.

I couldn't sleep. I longed to leave the earth. "Dear God,

please forgive me for asking you this, but rather than let someone who loves life get cancer, let me have cancer instead," I begged. "There are so many little kids sick with leukemia. Please, take the sickness away from one of them and give it to me. I don't want to be here anymore." Feeling hopeless and lost, I began to cry great sobs of despair. I didn't hear my bedroom door open.

"Angel, what is it?" mom asked, frightened.

"Oh, mom, they hate me again. I'm a failure. Please, please don't tell daddy. I don't want to go to a doctor for crazy people. Please, mom."

The next day, despite my pleas, I was scheduled to see a pediatric psychiatrist named Dr. Graff.

chapter five

Struggling
for Air

The rain pounded on my window. I awoke from a dream only to remember that I was facing a nightmare in a few short hours. I pleaded with my parents not to make me see Dr. Graff, but they wouldn't relent.

"Daddy, please, I'll try harder. Don't make me see Dr. Graff," I cried, my stomach in knots. "What if someone from school sees me entering the mental health clinic? I'll die of embarrassment." The more I begged, the more determined my parents became.

"Honey, he's going to help you," dad explained patiently. "Dr. Graff is well respected. He's made a difference in many young lives."

My parents didn't understand what they were doing to me. Though they meant well, I felt betrayed. I knew that I would be under worse scrutiny with Dr. Graff than I was with my classmates. I wanted to scream. My teachers weren't making things any easier, either. Mr. Warren and Ms. Gorge had both said in a meeting with my parents that in their opinion, I had "socialization issues." Hearing those words from two such respected educators only strengthened my parents' suspicion that I was "abnormal."

"You think Mr. Warren and Ms. Gorge are right—that it's my fault I don't fit in at school," I said, bitterly.

"That's not true," mom responded. "Your father and I just want you to be happy. We need to figure out why you have such problems with other children."

"I'm just different," I said. "If I can live with it, why can't you and daddy? Why do *I* have to see the psychiatrist? I'm not the one who tried to lose her virginity in a walk-in closet before her thirteenth birthday. I'm not the one who threatened to kill another sixth grader. Why am I being punished when I didn't do anything?"

"We're not taking you to Dr. Graff because you did something bad. We want to find out why you're being rejected. And it isn't just that. You're sick far too often. You've already missed twenty-one days of school this year."

"Mom, that's not fair. I had strep throat, and before that, I had that really bad cold."

"I'm not saying that you're faking. I think you're secretly relieved when you get sick because it means you don't have to face your classmates," she concluded. "You're using sickness as your escape and daddy and I can't let that continue."

Mom was right about one thing. I was glad when my doctor diagnosed me with strep throat. Anything was better than having to go to school. Morgan Hills had become unbearable. Sickness was my safety net. I couldn't get beaten up or ridiculed if I was home in bed. Though they weren't saying anything, I also knew my parents were concerned about my emotional state. I was despondent. I no longer cared about my appearance. I hadn't washed my hair in a week. Even brushing my teeth was becoming an effort. I didn't give a damn anymore. Gradually, I began to shut out the world. All I wanted to do was curl up on the couch and watch old Judy Garland and Mickey Rooney movies, and pretend that Andy Hardy and I were actually friends. I had wrapped myself in a cocoon. Even my beloved aunts couldn't penetrate it.

"I'm not going," I declared. "If you want me to see that stupid shrink, you'll have to knock me out first!"

"That's enough," my father admonished me. "We're leaving in an hour."

We rode in silence to Dr. Graff's office. Though it was only a fifteen-minute drive, it seemed like hours before we finally pulled into the parking lot of the Southside Mental Health Center. A modern two-story white brick edifice with gray-tinted windows and large glass doors, it looked more like a corporate office building than a clinic.

"Come on, angel, don't be afraid. Mom and I are right here," dad said as he gently escorted me inside.

The reception area was cold and impersonal. Furnished in chrome and plastic, complete with linoleum pretending to be tile, the only magazines there were professional journals on mental illness—hardly the stuff to relax a first-time visitor. The nurse, a somber, middle-aged woman, greeted us at the front desk.

"May I help you?" she inquired.

"Yes, I'm Tony Blanco, and my daughter Jodee has an appointment with Dr. Graff," my dad explained.

"Of course, please have a seat. I'll let Dr. Graff know you're here," she replied.

There were several kids with their parents in the waiting room. A fourteen-year-old girl was huddled in a corner staring into the distance, both her wrists wrapped in bandages. Sitting across from her was another girl, pale and rail-thin, the outline of her ribcage visible beneath her sweater. Nervous and uneasy, she kept playing with her hair. A little boy was rocking back and forth, muttering to himself a few feet from her. How could I have ended up in this place?

"Mom, dad, please, let's get out of here." Before they could respond, the nurse announced my name. I froze.

"Step this way, Miss Blanco," she instructed, directing me down a long hallway. We stopped in front of a doorway with a sign that read: "Dr. Jack Graff, Adolescent Disorders." This was a horror movie come to life. The whole situation was ridiculous. I was lonely, not emotionally or psychologically disturbed.

Dr. Graff opened the door. A large, balding man with piercing eyes and a gruff demeanor, his tough-love approach to psychotherapy had garnered national attention. He was best known for helping stubborn teens who didn't respond to more traditional treatments. The school board had recommended him to my parents because they thought I required someone who could handle a "strong-willed girl."

"You must be Jodee. Please come in," he said, gesturing toward a worn brown leather couch opposite his desk. Dressed in a dark pinstripe suit, crisp white shirt, and burgundy tie, he didn't look like any doctor I had ever seen.

"Thank you," I replied, staring at the numerous diplomas adorning his wall.

"Your parents tell me that you're having problems at school," he said, reaching for a pad of paper. "Tell me what's been going on."

"I've never seen so many diplomas," I said, changing the subject. "How many colleges did you attend?"

"It takes a lot of schooling to be a psychiatrist," Dr. Graff said. "I did four years as an undergraduate, four years of medical school, and then years of specialized training, internships, and residencies."

"What's the difference between a psychiatrist like you and a psychologist?" I inquired, wondering why he was scribbling notes already, when I purposefully had avoided saying anything *significant* yet.

"A psychiatrist has a medical degree," he explained. "A psychologist has a Ph.D."

"What was your hardest class in medical school?" I asked, pleased that my tact was working. If I could keep him engaged in small talk for another forty minutes, I would be home free, or so I thought. Dr. Graff wasn't so easily derailed, however.

"That's enough, young lady. Stop playing games and answer my question. What's been going on at school?"

I began to squirm in my seat. I felt like a trapped lab rat.

"You can ask me questions forever, but it won't change anything," I proclaimed.

"Won't change what?" he pushed.

"That I'm *different*."

"Different how?" he persisted. His cold, clinical voice unnerved me. It was like being interrogated by the FBI.

"I just don't fit in," I whispered in shame.

"Why?" he asked. "It seems that being the class outcast is getting you an awful lot of attention from your parents. Maybe you enjoy that."

"How could Dr. Graff accuse me of something so horrible?" I asked myself. "That isn't true," I shouted, fighting back tears. "I hate that no one likes me. It's killing me that my own dad thinks I'm a misfit, and that deep down, he and my mom both believe it's all my fault!" I jumped off the couch and ran toward the door. It was locked. "Let me out of here," I screamed, furiously twisting and pulling on the doorknob. "You don't understand anything."

"Jodee, make me understand," he demanded.

Shaken and with no other choice, I sat back down and told Dr. Graff what I had been going through since my classmates turned on me at Holy Ascension. I described the incidents at Morgan Hills, and how I reached the point where being hit hurt less than being laughed at.

"No matter how much I talk to you, it isn't going to change anything," I explained when I'd finished. "Maybe it's making my parents feel better that I'm seeing a psychiatrist, but you and I both know that you can't help me."

"I don't know that at all," Dr. Graff replied, snapping his notebook closed. "I'm going to talk with your parents for a few moments. The nurse will take you back to the reception area."

As I walked back down the hall, I grew more agitated with each step. What was Dr. Graff telling my parents? I was only in his office for an hour. How could he profess to know anything about my problems or me after just one visit? I felt as if I were being studied by extraterrestrials, my emotions and thoughts probed and analyzed. I could hear their high-pitched, alien voices: *Initial lab results from testing of human specimen number 42556 indicate subject is defective. Recommend relegation to isolation pod.*

"Jodee, honey, don't you want to hear what Dr. Graff said?" dad asked, jolting me back to earth.

"Oh, daddy, I'm sorry," I responded. "I was day-dreaming. I didn't even notice you and mom standing there."

"Dr. Graff would like us to bring you back again tomorrow for some tests," mom said.

"What kind of tests?" I asked, feeling as if I might get diarrhea.

"They're part of the evaluation process," dad replied. "These aren't medical exams like x-rays or blood tests," he said reassuringly. "Dr. Graff is going to show you a series of scribble drawings, and ask you what you see. Remember the Cloud Game that we used to play when you were little? We'd look up at the sky and make up what the cloud shapes were, like animals and dragons? That's sort of what you're going to do tomorrow."

"Forget it," I declared. "I'm not going to be a guinea pig."

"Jodee, Dr. Graff wants to help you, but you've got to be willing to help yourself," mom stated firmly.

"What else did he say to you?" I asked.

"Only that you're very emotional, and it may be con-tributing to your problems with your classmates," dad replied.

"What do you mean by 'emotional'?"

"Now, honey, don't get defensive," mom soothed. "Dr. Graff explained that some children are emotional and hypersensitive by nature. He says they tend to overreact to things that the average kid would typically just shrug off."

"What? Are you saying that I'm *overreacting* to what's been happening to me at school?"

"No, angel, not at all. But Dr. Graff did say that kids teasing and making fun of each other is a normal part of growing up."

"Getting hit and spit on is *normal*?"

"Dr. Graff feels that you may be overdramatizing a bit."

This couldn't be happening. It reminded me of one of those awful made-for-TV movies about child abuse where a little girl is molested by an uncle, but when she tries to tell her parents what's been going on, they don't believe her. "He would never do that," the mother in the movie admonishes her daughter.

Every time my mom and dad watched one of those movies, they would carry on about how terrible it was that the parents thought the child was lying. "How can you be such fools?!" my parents would shout in unison at the actors on the television screen. But weren't they doing the same thing to me now? I could tell by the way my mom and dad spoke to me that they thought I might have been blowing my problems out of proportion all along. Forget the cuts and the bruises, the nasty notes, the mud-stained clothes. My parents had found the easy answer they were looking for. Their little girl wasn't a misfit. She was merely *theatrical*. All she needed to do was see Dr. Graff for a few more sessions, develop a thicker skin, and, one day, all this would be behind her.

"Mom, dad, yes, I admit I'm dramatic, but I'm not exaggerating how bad things are at school," I cried. "Dr. Graff is wrong."

"Jodee, he's one of the most respected professionals in his field," my dad said. "We can't just dismiss what he says out of hand. We need to give him a chance."

I knew there was nothing I could say or do to change my parents' minds. I had become an outsider in my own life. Who *I* believed I was no longer mattered. It was what my parents, teachers, classmates, and now doctors thought about me that counted. I was so tired of being a hostage to everyone else's opinions that I couldn't hear myself think anymore. My world had turned into a circus, and I was the freak.

I continued seeing Dr. Graff for a couple of months. Each session was like the one before it. He asked me countless questions and took notes. After the sixth week, he called my parents in for a family conference.

"Your daughter is experiencing stress-related symptoms. That's one of the reasons why she's sick so often. Her stomach problems and constant fatigue are stress-induced," he concluded.

They were behaving as if I weren't in the room. He was talking and my parents were listening and nodding their heads. I felt invisible.

"That's not fair, Dr. Graff," I cried, furious. "When I get sick, it's not all in my head."

"Jodee, how dare you talk to the doctor that way!" my mom scolded me. "You apologize right now, young lady."

"That's all right, Mrs. Blanco," Dr. Graff interrupted. "Your daughter is under tremendous strain. I'd much rather she vent her anger than crawl under the covers and hide from it. Speaking her mind like she did a moment ago is wonderful progress. It shows that she's toughening up."

I rolled my eyes. This was absurd.

"I'd like to put Jodee on medication to relieve some of her stress-related symptoms," he informed us.

Now they were putting me on pills.

"There's a new drug on the market specifically for adolescents called Verstran. I believe it will help her enormously."

"How long will she have to be on it?" my dad asked, his face etched with concern.

"Whenever Jodee feels anxious or upset, she takes one of the pills. It will calm her down. It's a mild drug with a short half-life, which means within a few hours of ingestion, it's out of her system completely," Dr. Graff explained.

"Is it addictive?" my mom asked.

"No, not at all. Most youngsters who go on Verstran are gradually weaned off within a year or two," Dr. Graff said reassuringly.

"Perhaps we should get a second opinion," my dad suggested.

"Daddy, please, no," I pleaded. "That'll just mean more doctors and more psychological tests."

"Mr. Blanco, I can certainly understand your concerns," Dr. Graff responded, grabbing a brochure off his desk and handing it to my dad. "Here's some information on Verstran. If you have any additional questions, please call this phone number."

"Thank you, doctor," my dad replied, passing the brochure to my mom.

"I don't think it's necessary for Jodee to continue weekly sessions. Her difficulties at school are no great mystery. Kids will be kids. I've explained to Jodee that she needs to stop taking everything her classmates say and do so seriously, and to loosen up a bit. You're a lovely, talented young woman," Dr. Graff said to me, smiling. "You're going to be fine."

My parents were relieved. I could see it in their eyes. I knew they were living in fantasyland. Dr. Graff hadn't done anything. I was still the outcast at Morgan Hills. Nothing had changed.

Earlier in the week, our class had gone on a field trip to the Museum of Natural History. One of the exhibits consisted of creatures deformed by the effects of pollution, such as a frog with two heads. These mutants were preserved in large beakers and tanks filled with formaldehyde. "Hey, you guys, look—it's Blanco's relatives!" one of the boys from my class yelled to a group of his friends. They all burst into laughter.

That evening, when I got home from the field trip, I wanted to tell my parents what had happened, and I longed for them to hug and comfort me. I couldn't. Home and family were no longer my refuge. I'd learned that confiding in adults was more likely to bring pain than relief. Whatever I said would be reported back to Dr. Graff, and I was afraid he would put me on stronger medication. Stress wasn't the culprit. I was angry and lonely. How could a pill fix that?

I turned to my safest companion, my journal. It was the only place where I could honestly express how I felt without the fear of being judged by people who I no longer trusted. Writing saved me from being swallowed by sorrow. I discovered solace in composing poems. The language of poetry gave me a way to transform my hurt and wrath into symbols and images that I could control. When my classmates snickered at me or whispered unkind names behind my back in study hall, I closed myself off from them by writing a poem and immersing myself in the soothing sound of the pen darting across the page.

One afternoon, while waiting for my mom to pick me up from school for an appointment with Dr. Graff, one of my classmates pulled an indelible black magic marker out of her bookbag, and while her friend held me down, she began scribbling obscenities on my arm. When they saw my mom's car pull up, they ran off giggling.

Whereas I used to close my eyes and envision being invited to parties and hanging out with the cheerleaders and the football players, now I fantasized about hurting people. I didn't dare tell anyone of my dark imaginings. Instead, I wrote them down.

Revenge

You all think you're cool, stabbing my heart—
Bloodsucking vulchers, ripping my life apart—
Thought you'd take a loser, feed on her pain—
But you're gonna pay—
I'm not running again.
Revenge—how sweet is the word
Revenge—seems so absurd
But justice will find you
She's just biding time
So suffer and bleed
Pay for your crime
Victims are running—
Frightened and blind—
Lost in a world that's sadly unkind—
The vicious and cruel have fed on their souls—
Left them shells—

Empty and cold—
Their eyes are full of hate—
They've vowed to get vengeance—
To defy their fate.

If Dr. Graff knew, he would only increase my treatments, a fate that I would do almost anything to avoid. Though I tried to remain optimistic, my wounds festered. I wanted out of this hell.

I went along with my parents and doctors in order to keep the peace at home. Whenever I complained of an upset stomach or a headache, my mom would give me another "blue pill." For weeks, I continued taking the medication, until, finally, I couldn't stand it.

"Mom, I don't want to take Verstran anymore. It makes me sleepy. I feel like the walking dead," I complained. She must have noticed how listless I was becoming, because surprisingly, she didn't argue.

"All right, angel, I agree. I'm calling Dr. Graff," she replied.

Mom was on the phone for a long time. I hoped I wouldn't have to undergo any more psychiatric exams.

"Dr. Graff says it's fine if we take you off Verstran, but he also said that you still need to be on a stress-management program," she explained. "He suggested that biofeedback might be the solution."

"What's that?" I asked, wondering what surprise awaited me next at the local funny farm.

"He says it's a form of muscle relaxation."

That didn't sound too bad. At least it didn't involve medication.

"He wants us to go to the clinic tomorrow after school. He's set up an appointment for us with the specialist," mom said cheerfully.

The next day, when mom picked me up after school for yet another consultation with a mental health expert, I couldn't help but wonder: Why are the kids who get picked on by the school bullies always the ones who end up being poked and prodded in psychiatrists' offices? Why aren't the bullies ever taken to psychiatrists? Why do doctors keep telling the parents of the victims that it's *their* children who need help? And what about the parents of the bullies? What is wrong with all the adults? It seems that if you are mean or cruel to another kid, that was "okay" because it was just a *normal* part of growing up. If you are on the receiving end and allow it to bother you, *you* were the one who needs help. What kind of logic was that?

As we pulled into the parking lot of the clinic, I steeled myself for what lay ahead. I had no idea what I was in for. By now, the nurse in the reception knew my family well. She greeted us warmly.

"Hi, Jodee. I understand you'll be starting biofeedback with us. You'll be working with Dr. Keller. Why don't you and your mom go right in? He's expecting you. He's in the third office on the left."

Dr. Keller's office was sterile and utilitarian. Most doctors I knew kept photographs of their family on their desks. Dr. Keller's desk had nothing but a few sharp pencils, a notebook, and a small stack of files.

A studious-looking man in his early forties, Dr. Keller was wearing a crisp white lab coat over a pair of Levi's and a

T-shirt. "It's good to meet you, Jodee," he said, extending his hand. "And you must be Joy, Jodee's mom."

"It's good to meet you, too," I said. "What exactly are you going to do with me?"

"I see you don't pull any punches," he observed, smiling. "Biofeedback is a way to help people control their stress level without the use of medication or psychotherapy," he explained.

"You mean I won't have to talk about things that make me sad like I did with Dr. Graff?" I asked, encouraged.

"Not at all. Why don't you come with me and I'll get you started?" he offered. "Joy, you can wait here in my office. It'll take me a few minutes to get your daughter set up, then you and I can sit down and I'll explain the biofeedback process, and what we'll be doing with Jodee."

"Go on, honey," my mom said reassuringly. "Think of this as an adventure."

Dr. Keller ushered me into a small, windowless room. It looked like a scene from the movie *A Clockwork Orange*. In the middle of the room, bolted to the floor, was a contraption that resembled the electric chair. "I need you to sit here," he said.

I swallowed hard, trying to be brave. He strapped me in and began hooking dozens of wires and monitors to my arms and legs. He turned on a tape recorder and placed an enormous headset over my ears, telling me to tighten and release my muscles as the tape instructed.

"Jodee, don't be afraid. The electrodes are perfectly harmless. They measure your progress."

He closed the door and left me there.

Other kids were hanging out with their friends at the mall or playing sports after school, and I was buckled into quackery's cockpit, "squeezing and releasing." While most people were watching science fiction on television, I was living its demented cousin, "psycho" fiction. At least it was better than having medication shoved down my throat.

I was twelve years old and on the cusp of womanhood. I was excited about reaching puberty, and looked forward to what I hoped my body would become. Many of the other girls in my class were already shifting from training bras to the real thing. It was the hot topic at school. I found myself comparing everyone's figures in the locker room after gym. I was aware that my development was on the slow end of the continuum. One day in the shower, what I thought was blossoming womanhood seemed out of kilter. One breast was smaller than the other. I asked my mother if something was wrong. She assured me that it wasn't, but felt we should see Dr. Kalen, my pediatrician, as a precaution. Dr. Kalen agreed with my mother, indicating that my condition was not unusual, and would correct itself within a year. He would be proven terribly wrong.

chapter six

Fragile

Hope

As the school year neared an end, my outlook brightened at the prospect of a summer without doctors. My parents had finally understood that the psychiatric treatments were doing more harm than good and that the best medicine for me would be a normal summer vacation. I was encouraged on another front, too. My father's company was prospering and he and my mom had just purchased a new home. We were moving to Pason Park, a beautiful suburb bordered by sprawling fields and wooded lakes.

We weren't sure which school I would attend in the fall. My father, concerned that it would be akin to running away, was encouraging me to continue at Morgan Hills, which had both a junior high and high school. My mom didn't agree. She wanted me as far away from that academy as possible, so she suggested that I go to the local public school. To their credit, they left the choice up to me. Since I had until mid-August to make up my mind, I decided to wait and see how the summer went.

Moving to rural suburbia was like getting splashed in the face with cool water after you've been in the hot sun for too long. The change was refreshing and needed. It renewed my family's energy and awakened us out of a quiet despair. Everything about the new place felt hopeful and encouraging. Our home was a constant flurry of activity. My grandmother and aunts spent countless hours helping my parents decorate and unpack. My cousins came over to use our swimming pool every day. It was a magical time.

Our neighborhood was full of kids my age. I was nervous and excited about meeting them. They often played softball in the vacant lot across from our house. I would watch them, longing to join in but afraid of how they would respond if I just walked up to them and introduced myself. One Friday, late in the afternoon, I was in my room listening to my favorite Shaun Cassidy tape when I heard the doorbell ring. I dashed downstairs to see who it was. An attractive woman, casually dressed in jeans and a sweater, and her daughter, a pretty girl with blond hair swept back into a ponytail, stood on our porch, holding an enormous basket of assorted fruit.

"Hello, I'm Joan Babson and this is my daughter, Emily," she said. "We live in the brown house on the corner and wanted to welcome you and your family to the neighborhood."

"Hi! I'm Jodee," I responded, pleasantly surprised. "Please come in. I'll go get my mom." I bolted up the stairs. "Mom, the neighbors are here. They want to say hello. Hurry!" I cried, pulling on her hand.

I introduced her to Emily and Mrs. Babson.

"It's a pleasure meeting you. We were all wondering who would move in here. It's such a lovely home," Mrs. Babson commented.

"Thank you. My husband and I feel blessed to have found it. Can I offer you a cup of coffee, Mrs. Babson?"

"Please call me Joan, and that sounds wonderful," Mrs. Babson replied.

"Emily, while Jodee's mom and I chat, why don't you take Jodee around and introduce her to the rest of the kids?"

"Okay, mom," Emily responded enthusiastically. "Come on, let's go!"

Walking and talking with Emily on that balmy June afternoon, breathing in the smell of fresh-cut grass and lilacs, I felt happy and safe. It was as if I had been in hibernation, and was slowly coming out of a long, isolated slumber, stretching my limbs, my eyelids opening to the warmth of the blinding sun. Though part of me was still suspicious that I might be hurt again, I clung to hope. As my new friend and I strolled toward the softball field, I started to believe that the harsh winter of my past was giving way to a gentler season of abundance.

"That's Jim," Emily said excitedly, pointing toward the batter. "He's thirteen and is starting junior high just like you in September."

"Good hit! Good hit!" shouted several of Jim's buddies as he slid into second base. With only five boys on each side, the ballgame seemed more like a practice than a competition.

Jim had curly dark hair and big brown eyes. Tall and athletic, he captured my interest immediately. "He's such a fox," I breathed, imagining what it might be like to French kiss him. I was getting tired of practicing on the life-size Shaun Cassidy poster hanging on my bedroom wall.

"Yeah," Emily observed, blushing. "He's definitely sexy."

"Let's take a break!" shouted another player, jolting our attention back to the game. Lanky with well-defined muscles and a mane of thick black hair, he was clad in a faded denim jacket and tight blue jeans. He reminded me of Fonzie from the television show *Happy Days*.

"Who's that?" I asked.

"That's Jim's brother, Sam," Emily gushed. "He's a sopho-more in high school. All the girls have a huge crush on him."

"Add me to that list!"

"Jodee, you're just boy crazy," Emily observed with a smile.

"No, just aware of the cute ones," I said, laughing.

"Hey guys, look who's here," Jim announced, gesturing at Emily and me to come over.

They're going to like you. Don't be afraid.

"Hi, you must be from the new house," Jim said, smiling. "Emily said she might bring you over today."

"I'm really glad she did. My family only moved in last week. I saw you all playing softball, but felt weird about just coming over without knowing anybody," I confessed.

"Yeah, I would have felt weird doing something like that, too. It's hard when you're new," he sympathized, his brown eyes making me tingle. *Dear God, please don't let me say or do anything stupid.*

"Tell me about it," I replied, wondering if this was what falling in love felt like.

"My brother and I built this really cool treehouse. Emily can introduce you to everybody, and then we'll show it to you."

"That'd be great," I said.

For the next half-hour, I met the other kids who lived in the neighborhood. Rickie (who was my age), his younger brother Robbie, and their three younger sisters lived across the street from Jim and Sam. Their parents were avid gardeners, and their backyard was filled with rows of flowers and plants.

Greg, another boy in junior high, lived by the lake. He liked to go exploring, and often searched for snakes and frogs at night with G.I. Joe flashlights. He was also fascinated by dinosaurs, and invited me to join him and his friends on fossil-hunting expeditions after school.

Jason, who was also my age, and his two younger brothers lived several doors down from me in a modern ranch that reminded me of the house from *The Brady Bunch*. Jason, gangly and awkward, was often the butt of group jokes. It didn't seem to bother him—at least, that's what he said.

Kim, a tomboy with a daredevil streak, lived across from Jason and his family. She had a pool table and a soda fountain in her house and everyone hung out there in the evenings after their homework was done.

Kim's cousin, Reese, spent a lot of time with us, too. Diabetic since he was a child, Reese tried to compensate for his illness by being tough. I soon realized that it was just an act. He rescued injured birds and helped my mom around the yard. Reese had a good heart, but most of the other kids feared his temper. Their fears were unfounded, though. Reese's demeanor could be scary, but I had a soft spot for him because I knew what it was like to be misunderstood.

Paul, a freshman and the star of his high school wrestling team, lived directly across the street from Kim. I had an instant crush on Paul, too. His family, like mine, adored animals. They had a little cur named Duke. When Paul went jogging each morning as part of his wrestling training, Duke tagged along beside him. Paul made me feel protected from the moment we met.

"Jodee, hold my hand so you don't fall," Paul said, stretching out his arm to me as I nervously climbed my way to the treehouse. Nestled in a giant willow with long branches and rich green leaves, it looked like something out of *Huckleberry Finn*. I had never been in a treehouse before, and I was engrossed in the adventure.

"This is so neat," I remarked, hoisting myself onto the large wooden planks that served as the floor. "How long did it take you guys to build?"

"About four months," Sam responded proudly.

"This is secret," Jim chimed in. "None of our parents knows it's here."

"Your secret's safe with me," I assured him.

"Now it's your secret, too."

My heart skipped a beat.

That summer, I started to heal. My new companions and I delighted in the simple pleasures of being teenagers. Together, we went hiking and exploring in the woods, collecting rocks and arrowheads. We swam, played softball and touch football, and held relay races. On rainy afternoons, the girls listened to records, laughing and gossiping about our favorite rock stars, spending hours cutting out pictures from fan magazines and pasting them into scrapbooks dedicated to our idols.

Whenever one of us had a problem, we'd all gather at the treehouse to discuss it. The treehouse was our escape from the adult world, a place where we could share our secrets without fear of judgment or punishment. We pondered the mysteries of sex and dating, talked about what we would be when we grew up, and vented the angst and frustrations of adolescence.

I was one of the lucky ones. My parents had a good marriage. Some of my new friends weren't so fortunate. Jason's parents were constantly bickering. His home life was like a war zone. I felt sorry for him. He had nowhere to turn except to us. Though we did our best to cheer him up, he needed a kind of love and support that we couldn't give him.

Our parents took turns driving us to the mall or to the movies and out for pizza on the weekends. We also went to an old-fashioned ice-cream parlor a few miles down the road. The same family had owned it for three generations and they made the ice cream on the premises, using cream from a local dairy. Every Friday, my mom loaded my friends and me into her Buick and treated us all to a cone, the kind where the ice cream was packed so thick inside that it dripped from the bottom. The interior of her car would be sticky with melted ice cream by the time we got home, but she never seemed to mind. Her daughter was experiencing life as a "normal, healthy" teen, and nothing could have made her happier.

I felt sorry for Reese on those Fridays. Ice cream was definitely not part of his diet. I didn't want him to feel excluded, though, so my mom and I did a little research and found a sweet shop a few miles away that sold sugar-free candy. Every week, after we left the ice-cream parlor, we swung by the candy shop. Reese was thrilled. After a while, some of the girls even started eating the sugar-free candy.

Over the summer, Jim and I became inseparable friends. Every morning, I would look out my window to see if Jim's garage door was open. If it was, that was my sign that he was on his bike and on his way over. It was my morning ritual. After Jim arrived, my mom would make us breakfast, and then we'd be off to hang out with the gang the rest of the day. At dusk, he and I would often walk down by the creek. We could talk about anything with each another. I explained to Jim what I'd been through with my former classmates. He knew about Dr. Graff, the crazy biofeedback, and how I longed to be accepted by the kids in junior high. It was a welcome comfort to have a boy my own age to confide in.

I wasn't the only member of my family who was happy. The looks of concern that seemed permanently etched on my parents' faces for the past few years had been replaced with bright-eyed smiles. No more arguments in hushed tones about what they were going to do with their daughter, the misfit. A new day had begun.

My dad decided that he wanted to throw a 4th of July barbecue and my mom heartily agreed. It was time for the Blanco family to start enjoying life again. The bash was unforgettable: They turned our backyard into a kaleido-scope of colors, with red, white, and blue streamers and fresh-cut flowers of every shape and size adorning the patio. The pool water sparkled like a diamond in the setting sun.

All our neighbors came to the party. My parents made each guest feel so comfortable and at ease that many people who were normally reserved let their guard down; they surprised everyone with the spontaneous, silly sides of their personalities. I closed my eyes and soaked up the sounds and sensations around me: people laughing and splashing in the pool, the clinking of champagne glasses as new friendships were toasted, the smell of hamburgers sizzling on the grill. I drank in each detail of that remarkable night. Even as a teenager, I knew that happiness could be fleeting and that you should never take anything for granted, especially being rescued from loneliness.

Our 4th of July party was all anyone could talk about for weeks. "Did you see the look on my mom's face when my dad threw her in the pool?" Rickie recalled, giggling, one morning in the treehouse.

"Yeah, but at least your mom was wearing a bathing suit," added Jason. "My mom had on a silk blouse!"

"One that was see-through when wet," Emily remarked, holding her sides because she was laughing so hard.

"Ha, ha, very funny," he retorted.

"Don't feel bad. Your mom's got great boobs!" Robbie chimed in. I suddenly thought about my own breasts and wondered if anyone would ever refer to them that way. Almost daily, I would look at them to see if they were becoming more normal. My hopes grew dim as I watched in horror as the right breast continued to balloon outward while the left one remained a shriveled, hardened knob.

I decided not to think about that now. It was bliss to be part of a clique. My priority at the moment was to choose where I should attend junior high. I had to register in a few weeks, and didn't want the decision hanging over my head any longer.

"Hey, you guys, I want to ask you something."

"Yeah, what is it?"

"I've got to decide which junior high to attend this year.

I'd like to go to Northwest, but I'm kind of nervous about starting a new school again," I explained.

"Of course you should go to Northwest with us," Rickie remarked. "I thought you were registered all along."

"No," I replied, embarrassed. Their response was making me feel silly that I had been worried in the first place.

"Come on, you have to go to Northwest with us," Greg said reassuringly. "It'll be great!"

"Okay," I responded, turning my face away. Tears—even tears of joy—weren't considered cool.

That night, I told my parents that I wished to attend junior high at Northwest with my new friends. Pleased that I had made my decision, we quickly filled out the paperwork. A week later, my enrollment confirmation arrived in the mail.

I was floating on air. But my lightheartedness would be short-lived . . .

It was the last night of summer vacation. I was in my bedroom with my mom, choosing my clothes for the morning.

"And don't forget, just a hint of mascara, a dab of blush on your cheeks, and clear lip-gloss," mom said firmly. "No bright lipsticks or dark eye shadow. Understood? I'm going to inspect your face before you leave."

"I promise, mom. I'll make sure I look natural."

"Good girl. Are you nervous about tomorrow?" she asked. I could tell by the look in her eyes that she was more concerned than she was letting on.

"I'm trying not to be. It's not like I'm starting from scratch. The kids in our neighborhood like me a lot and they'll all be at Northwest, too."

"Now remember, angel, just be yourself. If anybody gives you a hard time, just ignore them and don't stoop to their level," mom said.

"What are you talking about?" I cried. "I haven't even started junior high, and you're already assuming the worst!"

"Jodee, don't be so dramatic. It was a little innocent advice."

"No, it wasn't. You think I'm walking into another disaster—that I'm going to be the outcast again."

"Honey, you're not being fair. That isn't what I meant. It's just that you've set your hopes so high and I don't want you to be disappointed. Which do you feel like wearing tomorrow? The beige blazer or your off-white sweater?"

"The sweater. I hate that blazer. It makes me look like an old secretary. And don't change the subject. It's *not* going to be like it was before at Morgan Hills. I know why I was ridiculed and picked on there. I acted too grown-up. I've changed now. You and daddy always told me to be a leader, not a follower. You were both wrong. What good is being a leader if you're standing alone all the time? This summer, I did the exact opposite. I was just one of the gang, and went along with stuff even if I didn't agree with it, and it was the best three months of my life."

"Jodee, I'm thrilled you've made friends here. But pretending to be someone you're not just to be accepted will hurt you in the long run. Which shoes, the loafers or the Keds?"

"The loafers. Mom, give me a break. You and daddy are too concerned about the future. I don't care about tomorrow.

Just let me do what I've got to do to have friends *today*," I said, wishing this conversation had never started.

"Angel, just be careful and promise me you'll use common sense and not be less than who you are."

"Mom, why do you always have to do this? Why do you make me feel like I'm letting you and daddy down just by wanting to be like everybody else?"

I felt bad for snapping at my mom. But I had learned that you couldn't be "gifted" and liked at the same time. You had to pick one or the other. At Morgan Hills, I had gone the "gifted" route and discovered that it was social suicide. My classmates sensed it. Being liked was all I cared about now. I felt that mom and dad were strapping an unreasonable burden onto my back by continually telling me I was special and encouraging me to always be the "bigger person" when something went wrong at school.

I was out of bed and dressed by six the next morning. Despite what I'd experienced in the past, I loved new beginnings. Hope was my favorite feeling, no matter how fragile the circumstances surrounding it. As I made my way to the bus stop, I saw Jim and Rickie walking toward me, waving. "Hey, Jodee," they shouted in unison.

This was great. I would be boarding the school bus with a group of friends, not facing it alone. Within minutes, everyone had arrived, full of energy and mischief. Jason, however, seemed sullen and distracted.

"Hey, Jason, what's wrong?" I asked, concerned.

"My parents got into another argument last night," he told me.

"That sucks," Rickie said.

I ached for Jason.

"You think they might get divorced?" Emily asked.

Hearing the "d" word was too much for Jason to take. He winced.

"I don't know," he answered, his voice cracking.

"Hey, man, you're a teenager now. Don't be such a baby. It's not cool," Jim commented, rolling his eyes and glancing over at Rickie and Greg.

I was becoming angrier with each passing word, but I held back the urge to say something in Jason's defense. By now, he was crying. I tried to comfort him.

"Jodee, don't coddle the sissy," Greg said indignantly.

"I'm not. But come on, we're supposed to be his friends," I pointed out, still trying to refrain from taking a position. I realized in that moment that it wasn't my parent's expectations of me that forced me to always defend the underdog. It was my own doing. I couldn't stand watching someone get hurt when I knew there was something I could do to stop it. You'd think I would have learned my lesson. Every time I stuck my neck out before, it had been disastrous: Marianne, the little deaf girl; and Dave, the nerd at Morgan Hills. It didn't matter who it was. Sticking up for people was the kiss of death. I couldn't blame my parents, though. It was who I was, pure and simple. I was just a fool or a glutton for punishment. Either way, I couldn't hold my tongue any longer.

Oh, great. Here we go again. Why can't I just leave it alone?

"Greg, it's easy for you and Jim to stand there and laugh at Jason. Your parents don't scream at each other day and night. Put yourselves in his shoes."

Silence. Jim glared at me. We'd never had a cross word

between us. I had never said anything remotely defiant to him. Mom was right—I was letting my need for acceptance change me into someone who might be popular today, but who I would grow to despise later.

"Jim, please don't be mad at me," I begged, hoping to retrieve his affection.

"Come on, Greg," he said, turning his back to me. "Jodee can protect the crybaby if she wants to."

The bus ride was a drag. I squeezed into the seat next to Jim, hoping I could talk my way back into his good graces by the time we arrived at school. "Jim, come on. You're going to give me the cold shoulder all day long for doing one stupid thing?"

"Jodee, look, if you want to be accepted at Northwest, and not have everybody make fun of you, you're going to have stop being such a wuss. Nobody wants to be around a saint with a big mouth."

"You're right," I acquiesced, gritting my teeth. "I won't do it again."

"That's okay," he said. "I didn't mean to get on your case so bad."

"Thanks," I said, relieved. Though Jim and I patched things up, I could tell that my behavior that morning cast seeds of doubt in his mind. I couldn't blame him. He was right. What I did *wasn't* cool.

"Jodee, wait up," Jason yelled as we exited the bus. "Thanks for this morning. I'm sorry Jim and Greg got so mad at you because of me."

"That's okay," I responded. "I know what it's like to be sad and scared. Believe me."

"I'm sure glad your parents decided to move here," Jason said.

"By the way, what would you do before when Jim and those guys got on your case about stuff?" I asked.

"Nothing. I walked away and tried to forget about it," he replied.

Why wasn't I blessed with the same wisdom?

You can't escape who you are. You can deny it, even run from it, but you can never, ever escape it. Most people were ashamed of the *bad* parts of themselves. I was ashamed of my *good* qualities. Maybe being strong would serve me well when I grew up, but it was destroying my life now. Why couldn't I be like other teenagers? Why did I feel so damned responsible all the time? Other kids didn't fret over the things that worried me. It had taken me an entire summer to prove that I could make friends. I would have to learn to live with guilt.

Northwest was a large school with two wings. The lunchroom was located in the middle of the building. Unlike Morgan Hills Academy, Northwest was sunny and cheerful. The halls were painted in bright shades of yellow, orange, and aqua. There were rainbows painted on the ceilings. It was a welcome change in décor.

As I searched for room 101, where I had first period English with Mrs. Wackles, I felt a sense of foreboding. Though I hated to admit it, the reason I had become so aggravated with my mom this morning was because I knew what she said to me was true. During the summer, I had practiced what I had learned from The Pitt Players about how to transform yourself into a character. I portrayed the role of the "cool teenager," rather than the real Jodee. Even though my new friends seemed sincere about liking me, I still had to act my way into social acceptance. When I was in a situation that made me uncomfortable, rather than choose to do what was right, I pretended our neighborhood was the stage, my new friends were fellow performers, and we were all in a theatrical production. It made it easier to do things I was ashamed of because I could pretend that it wasn't me who was responsible, but the fictional part I was playing. There were a few times when the kids were especially rough on Jason. I should have spoken up, but I didn't. Being in a clique felt too good. I didn't want to jeopardize that. But my neat little "this is just a play, it isn't real life" psychological trick wasn't working anymore. That's why I reacted the way I did at the bus stop.

Rickie, Greg, Reese, and Emily were all in my home-room. They had gone to grammar school with many of my new classmates. "This is Jodee. She moved in near us over the summer," Rickie explained to a couple of his buddies in the back row.

"Yeah, she's cool," Greg chimed in.

Instead of feeling comforted and reassured by the genuine kindness being shown to me at Northwest, I reacted like a Vietnam veteran with post-traumatic stress disorder. Images of Morgan Hills started flashing through my mind. Everyone had acted nice to me on my first day there, too. I took deep breaths to calm myself. I was overreacting, and not just about this moment right now, but about the incident this morning with Jim, too. Friends have fights, but that doesn't mean they stop being friends. I had to trust Jim and the others. They had never given me any reason not to. More important, I needed to fight the insecurities that kept rising inside me. Morgan Hills was in the past. This was a new school, a new start. Why, then, did I still feel like something was going to go terribly wrong?

Junior high was a new experience. I no longer had two teachers. I had a different instructor for every subject and physical education was also required. I wasn't too pleased about that. It was one thing goofing around with the kids in my neighborhood for fun—when I swung and missed or came in last in a relay race, it wasn't a big deal. Now, I would be graded on my performance. Worse still, gym class was divided into teams. If you didn't pull your weight, it wasn't just your grade that suffered. Your entire team paid the price. I had never been athletically inclined and was awkward in sports, especially gymnastics. I couldn't even do a somersault, let alone swing from parallel bars. At least it wasn't coed.

I was also self-conscious about changing clothes with the other girls in my gym class. My breast development problem was becoming more visible. So far, I had managed to conceal it from the other girls by not switching into a sports bra before gym and avoiding the showers. But what would I do in another year, when high school started? Showers after gym would be mandatory then. Mom and dad had taken me to several doctors, but they all said the same thing: "She'll grow out of it." I hoped they were right.

It didn't take long for me to get into the rhythm of junior high. My favorite class was creative writing. Our teacher, Mr. Bufert, was a lovable eccentric. He had the sweetest disposition of any teacher I'd ever had. He rarely raised his voice and he liked to make people laugh. He even gave students extra credit when they brought jokes to class. I was truly fond of Mr. Bufert, but some of the other students didn't appreciate his unconventional style. He had absolutely no idea that they thought he was peculiar and snickered at him behind his back. He took pride in what he falsely believed was a universal popularity that gave him the confidence to be uninhibited. Yet this uninhibitedness was the very reason he was such an effective teacher.

My first setback at Northwest came when my classmates wanted to play a particularly nasty trick on Mr. Bufert. One afternoon, A.J., one of the most popular girls at Northwest, had me in a predicament. She and several of her friends, including Kim and Emily, had been on a ruthless roll all day. First, they had replaced the head cheerleader's Bonnie Bell lip-gloss with a Pritt glue stick. The humiliated teen was still in the nurses' office, trying to soak off the adhesive with solvent. Then, still riding on a high from their morning mischief, they decided to stuff a bottle of Head & Shoulders dandruff shampoo into Mr. Bufert's briefcase.

I didn't feel too bad about the cheerleader. She had an imperious attitude and I didn't think a little dose of humility would do her any harm. But the stunt they wanted to pull on Mr. Bufert crossed the line. He struggled with a chronic skin condition that caused his scalp to flake. He was self-conscious about it, and always wore white shirts so it would be less noticeable.

"Hey, Jodee, he likes you the best. You do it," A.J. demanded.

"No way. We'll get caught!" I cried, desperate to wiggle out of this one.

"There's still five minutes before he returns from break. Come on," everyone urged.

"Jodee, it's just a prank. It's no big deal," Jim jumped in, his eyes twinkling.

"I can do this," I tried to convince myself. *Mr. Bufert has a good sense of humor. His feelings won't be hurt. Stop feeling so guilty. Remember what Jim said: "Nobody likes a wuss."*

"A.J., I'll stand lookout in the hall, and you do it," I whispered, the knot in my stomach belying my confidence.

Realizing that time was running out, A.J. agreed.

Five minutes later, our deed done, A.J. nonchalantly addressed Mr. Bufert as he entered the room. "Do you have our papers from last week? I'm anxious to see my grade," she gushed.

"Certainly, A.J. I wasn't going to pass them out until the end of class, but since you're so eager, we can do it now," he replied, pleased to see such enthusiasm over a homework assignment.

As he reached into his briefcase, he suddenly stopped, looking puzzled. Giggles exploded from the back of the room.

"I can't stand the suspense," A.J. whispered in my ear, excited. I wanted to throw up, but just kept right on smiling. I was not going to be the outcast again, bloody and defeated, sitting on the sidelines. Social acceptance was a battlefield riddled with landmines. I was a soldier who had to survive and Mr. Bufert's dignity was a casualty of war.

"What's this?" he asked, shaking his head, holding up the blue-and-white bottle of Head & Shoulders. "I give you people extra credit if you bring a joke *into* class, not for making a joke *out of* someone," he said, his voice weak with humiliation and shock. He suddenly realized that his beloved students didn't adore him at all—they disdained him. "I'm not going to say anything more about this," he added, his words tinged with the sadness of one whose illusions have been completely shattered.

I wanted to crawl inside a foxhole and die. I guess I wasn't cut out for war. Everyone in class thought I was so cool. Why couldn't I just revel in it? The truth stank. It was either be liked by everyone but hate yourself, or respect yourself and be hated by everyone. What a choice. I didn't know how much longer I could keep up this charade. Teenagers are perceptive. Eventually, my classmates would figure out that my "coolness" was an act.

With each passing day, maintaining my summer friendships became more difficult. I was so tired of pretending to be someone I wasn't just to ensure my social status at school. As seventh grade turned into eighth, my resolve weakened.

⁂

"Something seems to have gone out of Mr. Bufert ever since we pulled our dandruff trick last year," Emily observed one afternoon, her words sounding almost regretful. I'd noticed it, too—the joy and spontaneity that most of his students enjoyed was gone. But I dismissed the idea, not wanting to believe it.

According to my companions, that was nothing. "Wait until we *really* start having fun," they'd tell me by the lockers, in between periods. I'd respond with the requisite conspiratorial chuckle, promise to hang out after school, and then make my way to class. I was a member of the in-crowd. Popularity was all that mattered now.

Gradually, I began to cave in. Try as I might, my old self occasionally popped to the surface, almost making it seem as if I had a strange form of Tourette's syndrome. My friends and I would be in the middle of teasing Adam, the class geek, behind his back, when, all of a sudden, I'd say something like, "Come on, you guys, we're being really mean. Why don't we talk about something else?" It was as if I had involuntary twitches of conscience. Why couldn't personal morality be like a light switch? You could turn it off whenever you wanted, and after a while, you just adjusted to the dark.

At first, no one thought much of my outbursts. They'd warn me, as Jim had, about the perils of being a wuss, then move onto other, more important subjects, such as curfews, rock stars, and rumors. For months, I existed between being liked and being a jerk. I hated it, but it was still better than crying myself to sleep because I had no friends, or sneaking upstairs after school and washing the mud off my clothes so my parents wouldn't know I was the school outcast. Life was a balance. Finding that balance was proving to be an arduous proposition.

My other problem was that I didn't want to disappoint my family. My mom and dad had waited so long to see me happy. They were enjoying my social success more than me. Their relief was palpable. They were so pleased to see me engaging in typical teenage fun that they weren't even hassling me about the dip in my grades. I had gone from As to Cs and had not heard a peep from them. How could I tell my mom and dad that if they saw me in action at school, their pleasure wouldn't last long?

Frightened and confused, I decided to ask my grandmother for advice. She and my grandfather were living with us now in an extension my parents had built onto the house. Though I sometimes thought my grandmother was a Pollyanna, I trusted her instincts. As I confessed my horrible behavior, there were moments when I felt so ashamed that I didn't think I could say another word. She held my hand and encouraged me to continue. Two hours later, when there was nothing left for me to tell, my grandmother spoke.

"Jodee, you can overcome sadness, loneliness, even terrible loss. But guilt goes with you to the grave."

She put into words what I already knew but didn't want to face. It was the jolt I needed. When I went to bed, I vowed that the next day, I would abandon the sham.

That's when I learned firsthand the meaning of the term *domino effect*. Once I started refusing to conform to the whims and demands of the cool crowd, everything tumbled in on me. The friendships that had pulled me out of a lonely place and had given me a new lease on life began to disintegrate. It was as if my classmates had been under a magic spell that I had suddenly broken. One by one, they drifted away. The fact that I was doing the right thing was no comfort. The reclamation of my self-respect was supposed to be my reward, but instead, it was turning out to be a miserable booby prize.

My classmates jumped on any excuse to stick it to me. One afternoon in biology class, we were supposed to dissect a fetal pig. Though I had steeled myself to the inevitability of the task, the stench of formaldehyde and the sound of tearing plastic as the students extricated the tiny cadavers from their casing was more than I could stand. I couldn't make myself do it. I loved animals, and this was too much for me to stomach. I raised my hand and told Mr. Blatt, our teacher, that I would be happy to do any extra credit he required, but that I wasn't going to cut open an unborn baby animal. My classmates snickered.

"Ms. Blanco, dissection is a requirement of junior high science. You cannot pass this course without it," Mr. Blatt replied tersely.

"Please don't make me do this," I begged, fighting back tears.

"That's enough, young lady. I won't have any histrionics in this class. Either participate or I'm flunking you."

"With all due respect, Mr. Blatt, I'm sorry, but I just can't do it," I responded, shaking. Then I got out of my seat, gathered my books, and left the room. I could hear the laughter as I walked down the hall.

Not knowing what else to do, I went to Principal Gibbs's office. Mr. Gibbs was fair-minded and kind. He knew most of the students by name, and had an open-door policy. When he saw me come in, my eyes red and swollen from crying, he was immediately concerned.

"Jodee, what is it, my dear? What's happened?"

I explained to him what transpired in biology class. He promised he would talk to Mr. Blatt. The next day, Mr. Gibbs called me back to his office during homeroom.

"I had a chat with your teacher," he explained, handing me a sheet of paper with several topics written across the top. "Mr. Blatt has agreed that if you do a fifteen-page paper on any one of these subjects, he'll give you the extra credit necessary to make up for the dissection. But you'll still have to attend class."

"Oh, Mr. Gibbs, thank you!" I said.

"By the way, Jodee, between you and me, I'm proud of how you handled yourself. One day, that inner strength of yours will serve you well." I hoped so. But right now, it was making my life hell.

As I expected, the ridicule started that day the moment I entered the lab.

"Hey, Jodee," yelled one of the guys in the class, ripping one of the fetal pigs out of its bag, and hurling it at me. "Want me to cut you some bacon?" The small pink corpse hit me in the chest, splattering formaldehyde all over my blouse. I stood there, motionless, too humiliated to speak.

"Maybe she'd like a pork chop instead," someone else shouted from the back of the room.

Before I could respond, Mr. Blatt walked into the room. When he saw the state of my blouse, he chastised the class briefly, then handed me a bathroom pass.

The rest of the afternoon dragged on unbearably. By the time I got home from school, I realized that I couldn't keep the truth from my parents. When I explained to them the situation at school, they were supportive. They saw what was happening to their friends' children who conformed to the crowd for acceptance. Some of them were taking drugs and experimenting with sex. Though my parents hated the idea of their daughter being an outcast again, it was better than the alternative. This time, they weren't questioning my will.

They were grateful for it. They even offered to transfer me to another junior high, but I was determined not to run away. That solution hadn't proved effective the last time, and my self-esteem demanded that I stick it out at Northwest. Besides, I only had one more semester to endure.

The hardest part for me was riding the bus to and from school. My friends from the neighborhood were following Greg and Rickie's lead. They turned on me and never let up. Every day it was more of the same.

"Jodee's a wuss, Jodee's a wuss," they would chant over and over. Sometimes, one of them would hold me down while two or three of them threw dirt and gravel on me. One morning on the way to the bus stop, I saw them scouring the ground at a nearby construction site and then stuffing something into their bookbags. Not realizing what they were up to, I continued making my way to the corner to wait for the bus. As they approached, Reese dug his hand into his pocket and extracted what looked like a small chunk of cement. He held it up for me to see, then pulled back his arm as if he were pitching a baseball and whipped it at me. I sprang to my right to avoid being hit, but I wasn't fast enough. I winced as it smashed into my shoulder. How could Reese do that to me? I had helped him feel included in our crowd by finding that sugar-free candy for him. Hot tears stung my cheeks. Suddenly, tiny, jagged hunks of mortar were being hurled at me from all sides. My hands over my face, I tried to run home, but the assault was too relentless. "Please stop, you guys," I pleaded. My knuckles and wrists were swollen and bloody. Red welts covered my skin. I didn't know which was worse, the physical or the emotional agony. My assailants, having had their fill of fun, finally stopped.

Reese came over to me with a sheepish look on his face. "Go away," I sobbed.

"We didn't mean to go this far," he explained nervously. "Do you want me to walk you home so you can clean up?"

"No, I just want to be left alone," I said, slowly straightening up. "I just want to be left alone." As I started to leave, I heard the sound of a horn in the distance. The bus would be here soon. Wincing, I hurried my pace. I didn't want the driver seeing me this way. I was already embarrassed enough.

When my parents found out, they were enraged and wanted to call all the neighbors whose children were involved in the assault. I convinced them to hold back. "Mom, dad, if you do that, their parents will punish them, and it will make things even worse for me. Remember what happened after Callie's party at Morgan Hills," I reminded them. "Please, can you just leave it alone?" They finally acquiesced, but told me that if one more incident like that occurred, they were going to the parents and then the school board.

After the attack at the bus stop, I kept to myself more than ever at school. Emily and Kim both felt guilty about what had happened and tried to make things right. "After all, the boys were the ones who threw the rocks at you, not us. We didn't do anything."

"That's exactly the point," I said. "You both stood there and watched and didn't do a thing to help me. You could have at least told them to stop."

"We said we're sorry," Kim retorted.

"It's just that nobody likes you anymore, and if we stick

up for you, the same could happen to us," Emily explained. "It's nothing personal. We still think you're okay."

They honestly didn't believe they were at fault. If the situation were reversed, I would have tried to stop those boys or I would have found an adult to help. They did nothing. To me, that made them worse.

Paul was the only friend I had left. We didn't see much of each other because he was on the varsity wrestling team, and it took up all his time. He had heard about the attack from his mom. Not long after, he invited me to one of his wrestling matches. I know he only offered because he felt sorry for me, but I was thankful for his kindness. I had never been to a high school event before and was excited to attend. He won his match. I was proud of him. Later that night, he took me out for pizza and we talked for hours. He wanted to retaliate against Greg and Reese and the others, but his parents made him promise he wouldn't. "I'll always be here for you," he said reassuringly as he dropped me off in front of my house. "You're like my kid sister. The next time somebody bothers you, they're going to pay," he said.

My evening with Paul bolstered my spirits. I was also heartened by the coming of spring. It was already mid-March and soon, I would be graduating. I assumed the worst was over, and that if I could just tough out the next few months, I would be home free. My optimism would prove near fatal.

A freak blizzard had covered the ground in ice and show. I was running late after school and missed the bus, so I called my mom to come and get me. One of the boys on Northwest's football team saw me as I was making my way to the front entrance to wait for my mom. I heard something and looked back over my shoulder. Fifteen football players were behind me. "Maybe they're just going to their lockers," I reasoned to myself. I picked up my pace. So did they. Then, I was being chased down the hall. I bolted out the door, thinking my mom would be there. She wasn't. Four of the boys restrained me, two of them forced open my jaw, and others began shoving fistfuls of snow into my mouth. I couldn't breathe. I flailed my arms furiously, trying to fend them off. They were laughing so hard that they didn't hear me choking for air. I couldn't speak to let them know they had gone too far. Finally, Jim—the same Jim who despite everything, I still had a crush on—yelled, "Hey, you guys, I think she's gagging!" With that realization, they released me and ran off.

I remained huddled near the bushes that lined the parking lot, shivering. I ached from the cold. It felt like a thousand tiny needles were piercing my skin. Numbness started to spread across my face and fingers. I began to scream. I no longer felt connected to my own body. It was as if this had all happened to someone else.

When my mom arrived, she found me lying on the ground, hysterical.

chapter seven

Glimpses of the Swan

"Jodee, what is it, honey? What happened?" my mom cried, taking off her coat and wrapping it around me.

"No!" I kept screaming, flailing my arms, still trying to fend off my attackers. "No more."

"Angel, it's all right, they're gone," mom said. Grabbing ahold of my hands, she lifted me up and gently led me to the car. Though I knew I was safe as I climbed into the front seat, I was still terrified. I couldn't erase the memory of not being able to breathe. When she closed the car door, I felt like a trapped animal. I was emotionally and physically exhausted. By the time we got home, fear was the only thing keeping me awake.

When we walked in the door and my grandfather saw the look in my eyes, he grew pale.

"What in the hell happened?" he asked my mom.

"I'm not sure," she replied. "When I got to Northwest, Jodee was lying on the ground, soaking wet, and shaking."

"Can you tell your grandfather what went on?" he asked lovingly. "What did those kids do to you?"

I recounted the events of the afternoon. "You poor kid. It's a good thing I wasn't there, 'cause I'd have killed them," he said gruffly, hugging me close. As I snuggled into his embrace, he stroked my hair. "Everything's going to be all right," he promised.

My dad was in New York on business. When mom called him and described the incident after school, he was outraged, and caught the next flight home. Late that evening, we had a family meeting.

"Honey, I think we should talk to the school principal about this," dad said. "The kids who did this to you should be punished."

"Dad, please, you don't understand. I've only got three more months before I graduate. If I get anyone in trouble, especially the football players, it'll only make things worse."

"Jodee, I understand that you don't want to be a tattle-tale, but this is very serious. You can't keep letting these school bullies off the hook because you're afraid of how they'll react. How will you feel if they hurt someone else and you could have prevented it? Believe me, if they're punished, they'll think twice about ever doing something like this again," dad explained.

"Stop pushing me. Don't you see what you're doing? If I go to the principal and report what happened, for sure the school will take action. That's great for whoever was going to be their next target. But it's disaster for me. No way, dad."

"Jodee, we were confronted with the same problem at Morgan Hills, and I let it go then because I couldn't stand seeing you more upset than you already were. I'm not making that mistake again. If you won't talk with Principal Gibbs, then your mother and I will," he stated firmly.

There was nothing I could do. Besides, dad was right. It was crazy to let these bullies get away with such cruelty. They should have to take responsibility for their actions, not to mention be thwarted from doing this again. Even though I knew that lodging an official complaint was the right way to go, the idea made me cringe. On the other hand, things couldn't get much worse. There was also the fear factor. Who could say that they wouldn't gang up on me again? I had given them control over me, and they knew it.

It was as if a notice were hanging on the school bulletin board: *Worried about your status with the in-crowd? Want to show your friends how cool you can be? Just beat the crap out of Jodee, laugh at her, and make her cry. Be sure and do it in front of everyone. That way, the popular kids can see how amazing you are.*

I hated myself. It was my strength that made my classmates pick on me in the first place, but it was my weakness that allowed their viciousness to flourish. What a mess.

The next morning, my parents and I met with Principal Gibbs. When I told him what had occurred just fifty feet outside his own office window after he had gone home the day before, he was shocked.

"Mr. and Mrs. Blanco, I can assure you nothing like this will ever happen again as long as I'm principal of this school," he said. "No child should ever have to endure what your daughter went through."

"Mr. Gibbs, please don't punish anyone," I begged. "Things will get so much worse for me if you do."

"Jodee, I can't look the other way on this one. If I ignore it, that's the same as condoning it. Not only would that be unfair to you, it would be bad for the school. I'm afraid I have to agree with your mom and dad here. Violence at Northwest can't be permitted."

It seemed as if everyone had power over my life except me.

"I know this must seem like the end of the world to you, but years from now you're going to look back on all of this and laugh," Mr. Gibbs encouraged.

"I don't care about years from now. It's today, and next week, that I'm worried about," I responded angrily.

Within two hours, the news that I had snitched had spread through the school. Jim and the other boys who had attacked me were kicked off the football team and suspended for a week. The team couldn't possibly win the intramural championship without its star players. The entire student body blamed me.

Every day when the bell rang at the end of each period, I froze with fear. Walking the halls had become an exercise in terror. "You better get a bodyguard, because we're going to beat you senseless," A.J. whispered in my ear one morning outside math class. Then she kicked me in the shin as hard as she could. After that, I didn't dare look anyone in the eye when I passed through the halls between classes because seeing their fury was too scary.

The teasing and taunting that followed were relentless; it was like being bombarded with tiny shards of glass . . .

"Look, it's the school brown-noser. Go spread your snot somewhere else, bitch."

"Next time, it'll be a lot more than snow that gets shoved down your throat."

"Hey, you guys, it's fugly, the ugly freak."

"Want to go out Saturday night? I hear old man Gibbs needs a date."

"Only three more months 'til graduation. I can get

through this," I kept telling myself.

As the semester progressed, I became lethargic. I went through the motions of going to school, but did nothing more. Sometimes, after my homework was done, I'd walk by the creek, searching for fossils. I would pretend that Greg and the other kids in the neighborhood were still my friends and that they were on their way to meet me. It was a silly fantasy, but it gave me a break from my loneliness, even if it was just for a few minutes. Once in a while, I'd climb up to the treehouse when no one was around. I'd sit and close my eyes, trying to relive the happiness I once knew there.

One evening, just before dinner, the doorbell rang. When I opened the door, I nearly lost my breath. Standing on my front porch were all the kids from my neighborhood. They hadn't asked me to hang out with them since last summer. I was thrilled. I was getting my friends back!

"You want to play softball?" Sam asked, smiling.

"I've got a new bat you can try," Reese chimed in.

Part of me didn't trust them, but I desperately wanted to get back in their good graces. As we made our way to the field, I asked, "Hey, you guys, I don't get it. I thought you hated me now. Why the change of heart?"

"We feel bad that we hurt you," Jim said.

"Yeah, Paul talked to us last weekend, and he made us see things differently," Rickie explained.

"We're really sorry about everything, Jodee," Emily added.

"Please be our friend again," Sam said warmly.

I was relieved to hear that it was Paul who had inspired them to give me another chance. He was popular and they respected him. More important, I knew that I could trust Paul.

"I'd love to play softball with you guys," I replied.

"I'll pitch," Sam announced.

"Jodee, you bat first," Reese said.

They had never asked me to bat first. I felt honored. I stepped up to the plate, took the bat firmly in my hands, got into the proper position, and readied myself for Sam's pitch. It felt like old times again. I was in seventh heaven.

"Hey, batter, batter, batter," Rickie and Greg shouted.

"Come on, Jodee, you can do it!" Reese encouraged me.

Gripping the ball tightly in his right hand, Sam pulled back his arm, ready to throw an overhand fastball.

"Wait a minute," I cried. "You're not supposed to throw it like that, you're supposed to throw under—"

Before I could finish the sentence, Sam hurled the softball right at me. It bashed my leg just above the knee. I winced. Everyone laughed except Jason. "That was really mean," he said sheepishly, clearly afraid of how Sam and the others would respond to his disapproval.

"Not half as mean as what we'll do to you if you say one more word in fugly's defense," Sam replied, cackling. Jason quickly shut up. Then, glancing in Jim and Rickie's direction, Sam nodded his head. As if on cue, they bent over, pulled down their jeans and underwear, and mooned me. "Since you like kissing Mr. Gibbs's ass, why not give ours a try?" they said, bursting into hysteria. Sam grinned, clearly satisfied with his accomplices' performance. Devastated, I turned and walked away.

What a desperate, pathetic fool I was. Time after time,

my "friends" had shown me their true colors. Yet, I still wanted to believe they were sorry for causing me pain. I was becoming just like the character of the battered wife in those cheesy made-for-TV movies about domestic violence. No matter how often I got abused or degraded, I kept going back for more, convincing myself that things would change, and if they didn't, it was my fault. What was wrong with me?

My knee hurt. I didn't want my mom to know how stupid I'd been, so I went over to Paul's house and told him what happened. "I'll kill them," he said, enraged.

"No, Paul. Please, don't. You'll only get into trouble, and they aren't worth it."

"You're going to have an awful bruise," he observed, placing an icepack on it. "This will at least help the swelling go down."

"Paul, Sam, and everybody said that you talked to them about me," I said.

"I told them they should give you a break, but that's all," he replied. "Why?"

"I feel like such a jerk. I was suspicious at first, but when they told me it was you who convinced them to be my friends again, I fell for it."

"Jodee, there's no shame in what you did. They're the ones who should be ashamed," he said.

Eighth grade graduation day finally arrived. I was proud that I hadn't let my classmates get the better of me. I might have been beaten down, but I wasn't out. As I held my diploma, tracing the edges of the crisp parchment with my fingers, I felt an enormous sense of accomplishment.

After the ceremony, my parents threw a celebration in my honor. My grandfather hung streamers and brightly colored balloons from all the trees in the backyard, and my grandmother decorated the garden with festive ribbons and bows. My aunts and cousins, as well as our close family friends, attended the party. Though I tried to act excited, in truth, I was exhausted. I longed to hide under the covers and sleep away the memory of the past two years. It was as if I had been held hostage and only just narrowly escaped.

I was also dealing with a giant pink elephant in the middle of the living room that no one was talking about. High school. I was running out of fresh starts. There were only three choices: Catholic girls' school; a prep school, which would be another Morgan Hills with a dorm; or Calvin Samuels, the local public school. I decided Samuels was the lesser of the three evils. Maybe high school would be different. Paul had told me that the students were more mature and open-minded than in junior high. I prayed he was right.

One of my childhood fantasies had always been to visit Hollywood, and see the places where my idols, Judy Garland and Mickey Rooney, had lived. My parents thought a vacation to Southern California would be a wonderful break for all of us. So, in mid-July, we headed for the West Coast for two weeks. It was an incredible trip. We stayed at a posh hotel in Beverly Hills. One of my dad's clients knew someone at MGM, and we were given a private tour of the studio.

The highlight of the trip was Grauman's Chinese

Theater, a strange and magical place where legendary movie stars left curious mementos, not photographs, statues, or autographs, but hand- and footprints in cement, most of them signed and dated. Some of the prints were so small that it was difficult to imagine the star having a physical stature any larger than that of a child's.

I kept searching for Judy Garland. When I finally found her tiny imprint, I knelt down and gently placed my hand over hers, pledging that one day I would return to this very spot as someone influential. I also vowed that Mickey Rooney and I would become friends and that I would help him achieve something important. I would be somebody. Someone who was respected and admired, who was invited to the exclusive parties and social events. People would rely on my opinion and seek my advice. One day, I would be that swan that my parents and doctors had told me about. It was just a matter of time. No matter what loomed ahead for me at Calvin Samuels High School, there were wonders waiting for me later, and I would appreciate them all that much more if I suffered to reach them.

When we returned from California, my former drama teacher from Northwest, Mr. Palmerton, called. Every summer, the arts commission, in conjunction with the school board of Illinois, sponsored a statewide dramatic performance tournament. It was one of the most prestigious programs of its kind in the country. Mr. Palmerton asked if I'd like to enter the Dramatic Interpretation category. Everyone at school knew that he had long wanted to have one of his students enrolled in this competition, but was waiting for the "right one."

"It will mean a lot of hard work, but I think we have a chance of winning," Mr. Palmerton said encouragingly. "What do you say?"

I was so honored he had chosen me to represent our school district. "Oh, Mr. Palmerton, are you kidding? Of course I want to do it!" I exclaimed.

We chose Edgar Lee Masters's *Spoon River Anthology* as my material. This compilation of poems is told from the perspective of the dead standing over their graves, reflecting back on their lives. It was a daunting challenge. I had to memorize and perform four five-minute monologues, each in the guise of a different character. The only prop I had was a large black scarf. I practiced with Mr. Palmerton three hours a day, Monday through Friday, for the entire month of August. I loved rehearsing. It was exhilarating and became a healthy release for the pain and anger swirling inside me.

The morning of the competition, my house was like a mall on Saturday, bustling with activity. Family and friends popped in to wish me well. The tournament, which was being held in a high school gymnasium, was two hours from my home. My parents, grandparents, and I rode in one car, and behind us, all my aunts and uncles followed us, caravan style. People must have thought we were a funeral procession or a wedding party. When we pulled into the school parking lot and walked into the gymnasium, the security guard was befuddled by the large entourage that had accompanied me. My relatives took up an entire row of bleachers. All my great-aunts were clutching their rosaries, saying novenas. My mom and dad were pale. Mr. Palmerton kept pacing the floor. I was the only one who wasn't nervous. Just as when my dad and I did karaoke at family gatherings, I couldn't wait to get in front of the microphone. I loved pretending to be these characters and inhabit someone else's reality, because it allowed me to escape who I was.

There were five judges, all of whom were theater professors at major universities. They were seated at a large oblong table at the base of the stage. Twenty-five contestants were scheduled to perform. I was slotted toward the end, at number twenty. As I watched each of my competitors' presentations, I grew more anxious. Their talent was apparent. The material they chose covered a range of periods and styles, from ancient Greek tragedies and Shakespearean comedies to Russian plays and contemporary American dramas. One of my competitors, a petite girl with large blue eyes and a sultry voice, did a scene from Tennessee Williams's *A Streetcar Named Desire*. I could feel my confidence wane. How could I top that?

When my name was called, I stepped gingerly onto the stage. I closed my eyes, inhaled deeply, and imagined that I was no longer Jodee Blanco; I was now Amelia Garrick, a petty, small-town social climber destroyed by her rival. I removed the black scarf from my neck, flung it across my shoulders like an expensive ermine wrap, tossed back my hair, and placed my hands defiantly on my hips. Then, I dug inside my psyche, reaching for every bit of anger I'd ever felt toward my classmates, the doctors who had poked and probed me, the teachers who weren't there for me, and my own self-loathing. When I thought I might scream from the pain, I opened my eyes and began Amelia's monologue . . .

Yes, here I lie close to a stunted rose bush in a forgotten place near the fence where the thickets from Siever's woods have crept over, growing sparsely. . . . ■

When I finished Amelia's ghostly speech, I closed my eyes again, gently removed the scarf from my shoulders, wrapped it around me like a shawl, and changed into Mabel Osborne, a lonely woman neglected and abandoned by those she loved. I conjured vivid memories of the isolation and sadness of being the outcast. I envisioned my shoe floating in the toilet at Morgan Hills, and my bookbag stuffed with garbage. With each recollection, I could feel Mabel's character expanding inside me. When I spoke, it was as if the sadness in my own heart were emptying itself into her words.

Your red blossoms amid green leaves are drooping, beautiful geranium! But you do not ask for water. You cannot speak! You do not need to speak—Everyone knows that you are dying of thirst, yet they do not bring water! . . . ■

With each subsequent transformation, my confidence grew. I portrayed an adulteress wrongfully imprisoned for her husband's murder, then a mother mourning the loss of her unborn child. The more I tapped into the hurt of old wounds, the stronger the characters emerged. When I completed the last of the four monologues, I folded the scarf, placed it at my feet, and then bowed to the audience. For the next hour, I watched as the last of my able contenders gave their performances. It would be a close contest. At 7:00 P.M., a hush descended upon the gym. The judges were making their way to the podium to announce the winners. They read off the names of the third and second place winners. Nothing. My aunts' praying became audible. Had I lost, I would be a failure at this, too.

Then I heard it. "And first place goes to Jodee Blanco, who was the only contestant to receive perfect scores. Congratulations, Jodee! Please come to the podium to receive your trophy."

That evening, my dad bought a bottle of Dom Perignon. When we arrived home, my family toasted my victory. High school would be all right. I had proven today that there really was room for me in this world. I *could* succeed after all.

As we clinked champagne glasses, we heard a deafening bang come from the backyard, as if a shotgun had been fired. My dad and grandfather rushed to see what happened. As they opened the back door, they heard a strange crackling noise, and saw tendrils of smoke rising from a small burned patch on the lawn. "Somebody threw a lit cherry bomb into the garden," my cousin yelled. "One of us could have been blinded if we were anywhere near that thing when it went off."

Just then, I saw the garage door at Sam's house close, and the upstairs lights go on. Mom noticed it, too. "Jodee, don't let them spoil your special day. They're just jealous of your talent," she said. I tried to put the unpleasant incident out of my mind. But I couldn't shake the feeling that it was a warning of things to come.

chapter eight

High School

Horrors

Freshman Year

I struggle to concentrate as Ms. Raine describes our first lab experiment for her biology class. Though I try to take notes, I cannot stop staring at the back of Tyler's head. His thick, shoulder-length hair beckons to be touched. He sits so close to me that I can smell his shampoo. I close my eyes and imagine my face in the nape of his neck, breathing in the scent of his skin and the hint of cigarette smoke clinging to his T-shirt.

"The substance most important to sustaining life, Jodee, can you tell us what it is?" Ms. Raine asks, jolting me out of my romantic fog.

"What? Oh, yes . . . um, what was the question?"

"The stuff of life dear, what is it?" she repeats.

"Water, it's got to be water, right?"

"Good. And what's the chemical symbol?"

"That's easy," I reply. "H_2O."

Though I smile and pretend to be interested, my mind drifts once more, this time to my favorite movie that I saw over summer break, *Grease* with John Travolta and Olivia Newton-John. I fantasize that I am Sandy, the character portrayed by Olivia Newton-John. The new girl at school, Sandy is initially rejected by the cool crowd, who think she's nothing but a goody two-shoes. Even more heart-breaking, she discovers that Danny, the kind, sweet boy who she fell in love with over the summer, is their leader. He turns his back on her when school starts because he doesn't want his friends to know that he cares about someone they've deemed unacceptable. Eventually, Sandy not only wins the affection and respect of Danny's clique, but some of the girls in her class give her a makeover that transforms her into the epitome of cool. In the end, she gets Danny back, and becomes the most popular girl in her graduating class.

As I drift deeper into my daydream, Ms. Raine begins to sound like the adults in those old Charlie Brown cartoons, as if she's talking through a kazoo. Though I try to focus on biology, it's no use. The pull of the fantasy is too strong. It also protects me from facing an unpleasant reality. A lot of the kids I went to junior high with have also matriculated to Samuels. I thought I could handle it. I was naïve. I underestimated the enemy. I didn't realize that overcoming the bias of a handful of freshmen would be this tough. It also never occurred to me how much influence they could have on my new classmates.

Biology period is the worst, with A.J., Greg, Emily, and several others from Northwest sitting just a few feet away. Each afternoon, they gang up on me, riding me about what I'm wearing or how I've done my hair. They snicker behind my back, sharing jokes with the rest of the class about how I refused to dissect the pig in Mr. Blatt's class, or how I went crying to the principal over a silly "snowball fight." I feel as if I'm trapped inside a stereo that's playing a broken record . . .

"Blanco, you suck."

"Don't be nice to *her*. She's gross. We hated her so much in junior high."

"Too bad you weren't a miscarriage."

If I don't find a way to stop them from publicly belittling me, their disdain will become contagious. I'll carry the stigma of being the class misfit again. At first, I make an effort to reason with them. "Come on, you guys, we're not in junior high anymore. Let's start fresh."

"Fat chance," they proclaim, rolling their eyes conspiratorially.

I know cruelty is currency in high school. It can buy power and popularity. My former classmates sense my desperation and amuse themselves by taking advantage of it. They need me. They're just as scared as I am about making friends at Samuels. They have to prove to the in-crowd here that they've got what it takes. I'm their best hope. All they have to do is make everyone see me as the outcast. Then they can say to the popular group, "We have a mutual interest. None of us likes Jodee." It confirms their social status. If I weren't so furious about it, I'd laugh.

"Hey, Tyler, I bet Jodee's never necked with anyone," A.J. remarks, smirking. "Why don't you give ugly little Ms. Priss a mercy kiss?"

"I'd rather suck on garbage," he replies, proud of his clever comeback. Clark, the class jokester and Tyler's best friend, turns around and gives his buddy a high-five.

I don't understand. Tyler and I ride the same school bus. He's never been unkind to me before. He ignores me if his friends are around, but that's because he's protecting his reputation. It wouldn't be cool for him to be seen talking with someone who's not a member of his clique. But when we're alone, he's really nice. I suppose I better get used to this. All the freshmen are jockeying for position now. This is especially true for people like Tyler, who have never known anything but popularity. The idea of going through high school without it is their greatest fear. If I can just keep my old classmates from Northwest at bay, I still stand a chance with the new kids.

"That's enough, Tyler," Ms. Raine declares, fixing him with an angry stare. "The next high-five I see, you'll sit in detention."

I sink into my desk. Here we go again. So much for believing I could make a fresh start at Samuels. The hardest thing about being an outcast isn't the love you don't receive. It's the love you long to give that nobody wants. After a while, it backs up into your system like stagnant water and turns toxic, poisoning your spirit. When this happens, you don't have many choices available. You can become a bitter loner who goes through life being pissed off at the world; you can fester with rage until one day you murder your classmates. Or, you can find another outlet for your love, where it will be appreciated and maybe even returned.

Samuels has a nationally recognized special education program. Most of these students are victims of Down's syndrome and other developmental disorders. They often stop to chat with me in between classes, to show me a picture they've drawn, or to sing a new song they've learned. They sense my loneliness the way a blind person can hear sounds the rest of us can barely detect. They possess a grace of spirit and clarity of feeling, for they are unencumbered by petty desires and shallow concerns.

Every day, the special ed kids endure abuse from many of the other students. They are mercilessly teased and called names such as "retard," "spastic," and "head case." These children are so innocent that they often don't understand the maliciousness of the insults. They smile in response, and offer their assailants a piece of chewing gum in return, thrilled that one of the "big kids" spoke to them. Many of the teachers turn a deaf ear. It reminds me of Holy Ascension and Marianne, only this is much worse. Holy Ascension is operated by nuns and priests who practice compassion. At Samuels, apathy is the norm. Most of the teachers here arrive when they have to and leave as soon as they can, doing the bare minimum. The special ed instructors seem to care more, but it doesn't make them any braver. They watch as their students are degraded day after day, but they rarely fight back. Nobody at Samuels likes to make waves. *Boy, am I ever in the wrong environment.*

Ms. Raine is still going on about H_2O. I feel a little guilty. She puts so much effort into trying to excite her students. But let's face it, water just isn't a provocative subject. The entire class is bored stiff. I wish she would switch topics. If my classmates grow too restless, they will pick on me to pass the time. *Come on, Ms. Raine. Pull something out of a hat.* No luck. In her own mind, she's on a roll. "There are a wide variety of pollutants in our water, as you can see from the photos on page one hundred of your textbooks. . . . "

I keep glancing at the clock on the wall. Only five more

minutes before the day is over. Finally, the bell rings. As I gather my books, I hear Tyler and Clark playfully arguing about which one of them Jacklyn, the hottest girl in school, would rather go out with. Petite with dark brown eyes and beautiful auburn hair, Jacklyn tries to look and act older than she is. She wears miniskirts, high-heeled shoes, and jeans so tight you wonder how she can breathe. Jacklyn's not only popular with the boys because of how she looks. She has a reputation for liking the backseats of cars.

"I'll bet you ten bucks that she won't be able to resist me," Tyler declares, pulling a comb out of his back pocket and running it through his hair.

"You're on," Clark replies, slapping Tyler on the back. I listen to their exchange, wishing it were me they were competing for.

As I make my way to the bus, I see Roger, one of my friends in the special ed program, stop Mark, the captain of the football team. Roger is severely challenged. His mental capacity is that of an eight-year-old. He also suffers from a disorder that has left him hairless—he doesn't even have eyelashes or eyebrows. His metabolism is impaired, too, causing him to be significantly overweight, and his muscles are soft and underdeveloped. Though he can speak in short, simple sentences, he has a lisp that makes him difficult to understand. Roger adores bright colors, and Mark's blue-and-gold football uniform fascinates him. All he wants to do is touch it. As Mark approaches, Roger reaches out his hand, and gingerly places his finger on the Samuels Hawks' emblem. Mark is repulsed. "Get away from me, you stupid retard," he shouts. Roger doesn't know what to make of Mark's angry outburst. Confused, he turns away, frightened that he made one of the "big kids" mad.

I go to Roger. "Roger, don't feel bad," I tell him, trying to soothe his hurt feelings. Roger looks at me with his bright blue eyes and smiles from ear to ear.

I now realize what Dorothy means in the final scene from *The Wizard of Oz*, when she says that if you have to look beyond your own front door for your heart's desire, perhaps it was never there to begin with. Would I like to be part of the popular crowd? Yes, desperately. Do I long to go on a date with Tyler and be invited to all the cool parties? More than words can say. But maybe those things aren't so important. Maybe, like Dorothy, I should embrace the love right in front of me and not search for some elusive dream that never mattered in the first place.

"Roger, will you take me to your teacher, Ms. O'Shea?"

"Yeah, yeah," Roger replies, taking my hand. As we make our way to his homeroom, I think about what my dad has always told me about having a purpose in life—something that makes you want to get up in the morning no matter what. I ask Ms. O'Shea if she would let me volunteer during my daily study hall.

"Please, Ms. O'Shea? I promise it won't affect my grades. I really want to work with the special ed kids," I tell her.

A petite, red-haired woman in her early forties, Ms. O'Shea eyes me with skepticism. "Are you sure you're up for this? They're great kids, but they can wear you down," she responds.

"Yes, I'm positive. Give me a chance."

"That's just the problem. These children need consistency. I've had volunteers before. They come for a few weeks, but then lose interest. I don't want that to happen again."

"It won't, Ms. O'Shea. Please?"

"All right, you can join us during your study hall. But just remember that it's a commitment and I'm counting on you to honor it."

As the semester progresses, I start to settle into a routine. I spend a lot of time with Noreen, my friend from speech class. My mom took us to Marshall Field's to get our faces professionally made up at the Lancôme counter. I couldn't believe the difference a little blush and eyeliner could make.

"We look amazing!" I proclaim, blotting my lips on a piece of tissue paper. "Can you believe it's really us?"

"I know, it's like we're different people," Noreen replies, unable to stop looking at our reflections in the mirror. "I can't wait for my mom to see."

"Me, too."

That night after mom and I drop off Noreen, I'm more pensive than usual. Concerned, mom asks if anything's wrong. "Jodee, you're awfully quiet. Did you get bothered again on the bus? I found spitballs in your hairbrush."

"What are you doing, going through my private things?"

"You left your hairbrush in the bathroom, so I decided to clean it. That's when I saw the spitballs. Honey, we've been through this before. If you're getting picked on again, daddy and I want to know."

"No, it's okay, mom. Really. As long as I keep to myself on the bus, it's not so bad. And things at Samuels are a lot better than they were at Northwest. Noreen is my friend, and I love working with the special ed kids. Speech team is also a lot of fun. I guess I'm just a little tired."

Mom isn't reassured, but I don't feel like talking tonight. After giving her a hug, I go upstairs and play my favorite Styx album on the stereo. As lead singer Dennis DeYoung's voice fills my room, I stretch out on the bed and close my eyes. The music flows through me, sparking my imagination. It's my version of Walter Mitty, but instead of being the central character in historic moments, I pop up as the leader of every clique at school; the star in a collage of my own mini-movies.

From jocks to junkies, I traverse Samuels's social gamut. There I am in my skimpy blue-and-gold cheerleader outfit, bouncing up and down with the rest of the girls on my squad (we are all a size six), rooting for the football team. My makeup is flawless and I smell of lilacs. Though I am jumping around like a kangaroo and doing cartwheels and hitch kicks, I do not have a drop of perspiration anywhere on my soft, creamy skin. I am head cheerleader, the grand dame of Samuels's cool crowd. We drive our daddies' sports cars and buy designer jeans with our mothers' American Express cards. We're hip, we're now, we're wow! And we never, ever sweat. *Go, Hawks, go! Put on a show! Let them know you're the mightiest foe. Go, Hawks. Raaaah!* As the fans whistle and applaud, the quarterback blows me a kiss from the field. My heart swoons. I shake my pompoms in response.

Cut to the girls' john. The smell of marijuana hangs in the air. I take another hit off my joint, pulling the smoke deep into my lungs. I stifle a cough. Whew, that was close. A real "head" (short for pothead), never chokes when he tokes. That's a rule. If the other girls find out I'm a closet cougher, it could mean the end of my status as Samuels's Goddess of Ganja. Unless, of course, I was a "jead" (a jock or a female athlete who's also a "head"). According to paragraph 8, section 3A of *The Official Code Book of Rules and Regulations for Samuels's Cliques*, "it is acceptable for a 'jead' to cough and/or hiccup during or after marijuana inhalation, provided that said 'jead' is in active training for her respective sport."

And the rock group Styx continues to sing, their lyrics pounding in my ears . . .

Fade to the school cafeteria. Move in on a close-up of me at a table with the "brains," straight-A students high on the fumes of their own egos. Clad in preppie attire, my hair pinned back in a bun, I am engaged in an animated discussion with my fellow thinkers about quadratic equations. As brilliant deductions come tumbling out of my perfectly shaped lips, the school's top chemistry student, who's sitting across from me, sighs, fogging the lenses of his glasses. We all giggle, for in our kingdom, fogging one's glasses is a sign of arousal, like when the Coneheads on *Saturday Night Live* rub cones. Tonight we're all going to the science lab to hear an extra-credit lecture on the mating rituals of the flightless birds of Australia. Tomorrow, I will be leading a sacred bonding ritual in which we stand outside the remedial reading room, pound our chests loudly and chant over and over again, "we're smart, you're not, we're excellent, you're snot."

Cut to the parking lot. A silent, lonely group of misfits are leaning against the bike rack. I am standing beside them. We are connected by our separateness. Our heads are down, we are trying our best to be invisible. Someone just spit at us as they walked past. No matter. This is our destiny. We are the outcasts, the nerds, the Eugenes from *Grease,* the Carries from the Stephen King novel, the kindred spirits of the Elephant Man. I ask Noreen if any spit got on her clothes. She says no, but I can see a small drop of saliva clinging to her button. I don't say anything. Better not to tell her.

As I lay in bed, my fantasies twisting and contorting into a montage of strange images flashing in my mind like silent movies, I realize that I am crying. Though I try to pretend none of it means anything to me, the truth is that like every other freshman at Samuels, I, too, care deeply about fitting in. I want to be a part of a group. Though the mature part of me knows that cliques are shallow and silly, and that I'm begging for trouble, the normal teen in me longs for acceptance. But which group? The brains are too conceited and cerebral. The "heads" and the "jeads" are into drugs. I've already been an outcast. They would be fine, except they're too busy hiding from everyone else to ever find each other. The cool crowd is all that's left. The cheerleaders and the future homecoming queens. Funny how my last choice is everyone else's first.

"Honey, can you turn that music down? Daddy and I can barely hear ourselves think."

"Sorry, mom. Right away."

I turn off the stereo and crawl into bed. As I snuggle into the sheets, burying my nose in my pillow, I wonder what's going to happen to me over the next four years. Mom says I worry too much, and that I should take one day at a time. I hate it when she talks to me in platitudes. I know she means well, but it bugs me. I am so tense, and it's only high school. If I'm suffering from stress now, what will my life be like when I have a career and real responsibilities? My head is spinning. Damn it. I'm never going to be able to sleep. The clock now reads 2:00 A.M. I have to get up in four hours. Tomorrow is going to be a bear. It's hard enough to get through the day when I'm well rested, let alone when I'm worn out from lack of sleep. Finally, I doze off. The last thing I remember before conking out is Dara's face from Morgan Hills. Why on earth would she pop into my head?

The next morning, I awaken stiff and irritable with a feeling that something's wrong. While I go outside to wait for the school bus, this weird sense of foreboding intensifies. "I'm just being silly," I tell myself. This is what happens when I don't get enough shuteye.

Riding the bus continues to be an ordeal. I still wait on the corner with all the kids from my neighborhood. Since the incident with Sam hitting my knee with the softball, they've lightened up a little. They don't punish me physically anymore. Now, they're just mean. I don't talk to them much, but I still like Jason. He and I are friendly. I don't blame him for anything. He's been picked on so much himself that I can hardly expect him to stick up for someone else. I don't think he's as strong as me. I'm also civil to Reese. Despite everything Reese did to me, I know he's not a bad guy. Reese never hurt me out of malice—it was desperation. He'll do anything to be one of the gang, even if it means disparaging a friend. Rickie's little brother Robbie is okay, too. He's not a saint, but he has expressed remorse for some of the stunts he and the others have pulled on me. I don't trust him, but what harm can it do to be nice?

The bus ride to school is the same as always. The cool kids sitting in the back seats whisper to each other, then burst into laughter. I know they're talking about me. I can tell by the looks on their faces. How I hate that sound. It's gotten to the point that when my parents invite people over and I hear them laughing over a conversation at dinner, it makes me cringe.

Today I have an important meeting with Ms. O'Shea. It's nearly prom season, and fifteen of her students, including Roger, are seniors this semester. The prom committee has said that the special ed seniors could not attend the prom. They believe that Roger and his friends would be an uncomfortable distraction to the other students. They also have "insurance" concerns. It's funny what pushes someone over the edge. I've watched all year as Ms. O'Shea sucks it up, seldom saying a thing when her kids are teased or disparaged. It's not her style to be confrontational. But this prom business has made her furious. She's asked me to share my thoughts about it with the school principal in the hope that as a volunteer in the program, my opinion will influence his decision.

The administrative offices are imposing. Large glass doors lead into a thickly carpeted corridor. Along the walls are portraits of famous graduates. The receptionist greets us curtly.

"Principal Evans will be with you in a moment, Ms. O'Shea. Please have a seat."

I feel sorry for Ms. O'Shea. She doesn't like discord. It's not her nature. "Everything's going to be all right. You'll see," I tell her.

"It makes me so mad that this battle even needs to be fought. My kids should be allowed to attend the prom. What they're doing is akin to discrimination. I'm not letting the school get away with this. I've put up with so much garbage from this administration, not to mention the student body. But this is going too far," she proclaims.

Just then, Principal Evans opens his door.

"I see you're all worked up about something, Constance. Let's see what we can do," he says, ushering us into his office.

"Dr. Evans, this is Jodee Blanco. She's a freshman here and volunteers her study hall hour to help out in the program," Ms. O'Shea explains.

"It's good to meet you, Jodee," Dr. Evans says.

"Thank you," I reply.

"Constance, I understand from the prom committee that you would like your kids to be able to attend this year's event," Dr. Evans says.

"Yes, they have a right to at least that little slice of joy. These kids have to work so much harder just to achieve the simplest things. They may be mentally challenged, but they're not deaf and blind. All everyone talks about is the prom. The decorating team is hauling streamers and equipment back and forth to the gym after school. My kids are aware of all this activity and they don't understand why they're not included."

"Constance, I understand what you're saying, but I'm afraid I have to agree with the prom committee on this one. It isn't feasible for your students to attend. The faculty will have enough trouble just monitoring the normal students, let alone students who need extra attention."

"Dr. Evans, I'll monitor the kids myself. I know the other special ed teachers will also volunteer."

"I'm sorry, Constance. My hands are tied."

"Dr. Evans, if my students can't attend Samuels's senior prom, why can't we host our own prom?"

"Please, Dr. Evans," I blurt out, saying a prayer that he'll give in. "It would mean so much to all of us. What do you think?"

"Fine. As long as you review all the details with my office prior to the event, I think this is a good solution. Now, if that's all, I've got another meeting," Dr. Evans replies.

Ms. O'Shea is beaming. When we get back to her room and she announces the news to her class, everyone claps, their faces lighting up with anticipation. After promising to return in a few hours to discuss the decorations, I leave for my next class. As I'm walking down the hall, I feel guilty. Though I'm pleased with Dr. Evans's decision and honored that Ms. O'Shea wants to me to help out, I'm concerned about how all this will affect my status at school. The last time I did something with special needs students that went beyond volunteering an hour at study hall or lunch period was at Holy Ascension. The scars from that experience continue to haunt me. What if it happens again? It's a risk I'll have to take.

During speech team rehearsal, Mrs. Adams comments about the prom. "Jodee, I heard about the special ed prom. I think it's wonderful. The whole school is talking about it. Please let me know if there's anything I can do to help."

"Thanks. I will."

Try as I might to concentrate on speech practice, I can't stop worrying about this prom. I love these kids, but dread the possible consequences. I can hear the popular crowd now. "Hey, look, everybody, it's spaz queen and the retards."

"Jodee, your mind is a million miles away," Mrs. Adams remarks. "You had better pay attention to what you're doing. The tournament is two months away, and you need to be prepared."

"I'm sorry, Mrs. Adams. Can we start again?"

The next day, Nadia, the head cheerleader, and her best friend Shelly approach me by my locker. Some of the football players on the varsity team have asked them to the senior prom. If you're a freshman and get invited by an upperclassman, that's considered the zenith of cool. My stomach is in my mouth. These girls are so popular. Do I still have a chance to be accepted by these popular kids who haven't discovered I was an outcast at Northwest? Steeling my resolve, I ready myself for the worst.

"We heard that you're connected to that special ed prom," Shelly comments, pulling a strawberry lip-gloss out of her pocket and applying liberal amounts of the goopy stuff on her mouth.

"Yeah, it's the week before the regular senior prom," I reply, wondering if she's aware how ridiculous her face looks.

"That's pretty cool," she responds.

Did I hear her right?

"You think it's cool?" I ask, utterly stunned. "Mark and those guys hate the special ed students. They're always teasing them. I thought you all felt the same way."

"Mark doesn't mean anything by it. They just freak him out because they're so weird," Nadia chimes in.

"I'd like to volunteer as a prom monitor. Do you think Ms. O'Shea will let me?" Shelly asks.

"Definitely. I'll let her know," I answer, completely surprised.

"Cool. See you in class," Shelly says.

Thank you, God.

As the big night nears, I begin to actually enjoy school. Public speaking is my favorite subject. Some of the kids think I'm a brown-noser, but that's because I'm on the speech team and our teacher, Mrs. Adams, is also the coach. Besides, Noreen is in the same class, and she's a supportive friend. English is kind of a drag, though. The instructor, Mr. Jobes, cares more about being liked by his students than about being respected by them. He rarely disciplines anyone. His daughter Lisa, one of Samuels's star athletes, is in our class. A high-ranking member of the in-crowd, she delights in showing off her superiority. Nothing gives her more pleasure than to test the power of her popularity by instigating verbal attacks against someone, and seeing how many others she can persuade to join in. Fortunately, she's left me alone so far. In her mind, I'm so far beneath her radar that I'm not worth her time. But for some reason, she has it in for Noreen. They're in the same gym class. Noreen tells me that Lisa picks on her like crazy, and gets the other girls to do it, too. They call Noreen "fatty" and "blubber butt." Noreen pretends it doesn't bother her, but I know the truth. Every time I see Lisa taunt someone in our English class, I imagine what it must be like for Noreen.

Biology is the real killer. A.J. and her gang won't let up. They've managed to inspire Tyler, Clark, and Jacklyn and her friends to join in their taunting. The special ed prom gives them all fresh ammunition.

"So, Blanco, you're the expert on the mentals. We sure hope they can take a joke," A.J. warns, her words tinged with menace.

"A.J., please, that's enough."

"What are you going to do, beat me up? I dare you." As if on cue, several of her buddies form a circle around me. Tyler, Clark, and Jacklyn watch the drama unfold, clearly amused by it all. There is nothing I can do. I can't fight all these people. I know I should try. But I'm afraid. Before I can respond, Ms. Raine walks in.

"Next time you won't be so lucky," A.J. whispers in my ear.

At Samuels, if you don't have a boyfriend or girlfriend, it's assumed that there's something wrong with you. On top of that, you're restricted in terms of who you can go out with. If you date someone from another clique, it can diminish or even destroy your position with the other members of your own group. For example, a cheerleader won't go out with a "head" or even a "jead"; a "brain" rarely dates a jock. Then you have the "in-betweens," such as the students who are into drama and art. Most of them forge their way into one of the mainstream cliques and end up dating their own. The computer nerds keep to themselves.

Samuels is also a jock school, which means you either participate in an organized sport, support one, or worship those who do. It's like living in Hollywood. Whether you're involved in the entertainment business or not, you better recognize it's the only game in town. Samuels is the same way. Hail to the almighty athlete or pay the price. And it's no picnic for the athletes, either. Their coaches push them far beyond what's healthy.

Paul and I talk about it all the time. His parents are so glad he's graduating this year. Last semester, his wrestling coach put him on a diet and exercise regime that nearly landed him in the hospital from exhaustion. Though Paul won't admit it, I think his coach also gave him amphetamines to help him get through the season. His mom is suspicious, too. I'm relieved for Paul, but I'll also miss him. He's been my protector for so long. What's going to happen when he's hundreds of miles away at college?

"Mom, hurry up. We're going to be late," I yell from downstairs, glancing nervously at my watch. Tonight is the special ed prom. Mom has agreed to be a prom monitor, too.

"Okay, Jodee, I'm coming," she responds, grabbing her purse.

We arrive to a flurry of activity. The gym is decorated in

a dazzling array of colors. Bright blue-and-gold streamers hang from every beam. Fresh-cut flowers arranged in large white vases sit atop each table. A D.J. booth has been set up behind the bleachers, where Shelly and her dad are playing "Hot Stuff" by Donna Summer. I wave to Shelly. She waves back, smiling.

When Ms. O'Shea sees mom and me, she comes running up to us. "Hello! You must be Joy, Jodee's mom," she says.

"Yes. And you must be Ms. O'Shea. Jodee enjoys volunteering in your class so much."

"Well, we love having her. Please, there's food and punch. Help yourself. The kids should be here any moment," Ms. O'Shea says.

What I see next I will remember the rest of my life. Roger walks in, handsome and proud, in a brand-new tuxedo. Standing next to him is his date for the evening, Sandy, a sweet girl who sits next to him at lunch. She looks precious in her flowing pink gown and matching shoes, her hair full of curls. Holding hands, they make their way to a table.

One by one, the rest of the students from the program arrive. A section has been arranged for the parents, all of whom are armed with their cameras and video equipment, eager to record this remarkable evening. Many of us fight back tears as we watch these kids enjoy an experience that too many other teens take for granted. Seeing their happiness fills me with a rare tranquility.

At one point, Roger grabs my hand, pulling me onto the dance floor. The song playing is Gloria Gaynor's "I Will Survive."

The next afternoon at school, everything comes tumbling down around me.

My social studies teacher, Mr. Horn, is physically challenged. His body is gnarled and deformed and he is wheelchair-bound. Though his appearance is shocking to his students at first, he quickly wins them over with his odd sense of humor. He's a good teacher, but sometimes I think he tries too hard to curry favor.

Mark, Nadia, Shelly, and several others from their clique are in my class. I've managed to hold my own with them by exercising self-discipline. Mr. Horn enjoys challenging his students to lively debates about current events. Even when I'm itching to participate because it's a topic of particular interest to me, I keep my mouth shut. So far, it's working. Nobody is calling me "teacher's pet" behind my back during class. I probably won't get as good of a grade as I could have if I jumped into the debate more often, but not being the butt of everyone's jokes is well worth the tradeoff.

Today, instead of a lecture, Mr. Horn has us watch a documentary about feminism. When the film is over, he wants me to return the projector to the audiovisual center. I'm not sure where the center is, so I ask him.

"It's next door to the rubber room," he responds.

"The *what*?" I ask, thinking I must have heard him wrong.

"You know, where the mentals are," he answers, pleased that his little quip gets a chuckle out of his students.

I can't believe what I'm hearing, especially from someone who lives with a severe handicap.

"You're supposed to set an example for your students, Mr. Horn," I respond, knowing that with every word that I am destroying what little progress I've had making friends in high school. "You understand better than anyone in this room what it means to be maligned. How can you be so intolerant?"

"Hey, Blanco, why don't you just shut up?" Mark says. "Mr. Horn is right. They're nothing but a bunch of rubber-heads."

I look over at Shelly. Why isn't she saying anything? "Shelly, you're volunteer, too. Why don't you speak up?"

By now, the entire class is glaring at me. How dare I embarrass one of their favorite teachers! "No wonder you're such a loser," Mr. Horn says to me, laughing. "It was only a joke. Class, what do you think? Maybe Ms. Blanco should consider going to another school. You obviously don't want to fit in at Samuels."

I slowly get up out of my chair, gather my books, and walk out the door, shutting it quietly behind me. Shaking with rage, I move with slow, deliberate steps to the tele-phone down the hall. I deposit a dime, then dial my parents' office number.

"Con Ship Maritime," a cheerful voice answers on the other end of the line.

"Mom, it's me. You need to pick me up from school right away."

"Oh, no! What happened? Things were going so well."

By the next day, the story of the incident in Mr. Horn's

social studies class is all over the school. Principal Evans calls me into his office.

"Jodee, what happened yesterday?"

"I don't want to talk about it," I reply.

"I need to know the truth," he responds.

Reluctantly, I relate the details. Principal Evans apologizes on behalf of the school, promising to talk with Mr. Horn. As I'm leaving the administrative offices, I bump into Mark and Nadia.

"What did you do, go running to the principal to complain about poor Mr. Horn?" Mark asks accusingly.

"For your information, I didn't say anything about Mr. Horn. But everyone at Samuels has such a big mouth that Dr. Evans already knew about what he said in class," I reply.

"You're such a goody two-shoes. Why can't you just keep your mouth shut?" Nadia hisses, moving closer to me and forcing me to back away from her.

"At least I'm not a hypocrite like your friend Shelly," I respond. "You're all alike. None of you gives a damn about anyone but yourself. You don't care about Mr. Horn. All you care about is staying on his good side so he'll give you a good grade."

It doesn't take long for the consequences of my actions to catch up with me. Not only are my classmates furious with me, but some of the faculty—who only last week raved about the special ed prom—are outraged, too.

"You should never talk back to a teacher like that," Mrs. Adams scolds me. "I'm shocked by your disrespect."

"Mr. Horn is a dedicated and talented man. What you did

was wrong," Mr. Jobes says, his words heavy with indignation.

Ms. Raine and Ms. O'Shea are the only teachers who come to my defense. The remainder of the semester is lonely. The scales are tipping against me. My new class-mates look upon me with wariness and disdain now. They don't understand why anyone would make such a fuss over one teacher's silly little comment. That's the kiss of death if you want to be part of the cool crowd. They don't trust anyone they don't understand or can't control.

During the summer, though I spend time with my aunts and cousins and try to keep my mind off school, it's no use. All I can think about is how close I came to making real friends this year . . . and then how I blew it.

I'm aware that being different is a social death warrant when you're fourteen. I didn't choose to be different any more than someone *chooses* to be gay or tall. You don't get to pick who you are in this life, but you can decide what you become. The popular kids like A.J. and Nadia, who are often so cruel, aren't bad people. They're just afraid of being alone. I think they sometimes secretly envy those of us who are different, not because they want to be outcasts too, but because they wish they didn't feel forced to sacri-fice their strength of character in order to be accepted by the group. Some of the meanest kids in school are prob-ably compassionate and sensitive on the inside, but they know that in order to be accepted, they have to be willing to be cruel once in a while. It's like flexing your muscles when you're a bodybuilder. You do it to reassure yourself that it's all been worth it.

Though I comprehend the dynamic of what's going on, it doesn't make it any easier to endure. In fact, it makes it harder. It's sophomore year. I'm more down on myself than ever because now I *know* the reasons I'm getting rejected, but I'm still unable to fix things—and that must mean I'm an even bigger failure than I thought. I hate who I am. I don't want to be this person anymore. My parents keep telling me that one day my fierce individuality will pay off, that I'll be someone important, that my innate leadership skills will enable me to do great and wondrous things. What a crock. Who cares about all that stuff, if right now, when I look in the mirror, I loathe who I see? Parents and teachers focus too much on the future. I need to be a normal teenager now, or all my tomorrows mean nothing.

As I sit in English class, the teacher is reading Shirley Jackson's short story "The Lottery." In the story, a crazy town holds an annual drawing. Each citizen has to put his or her name on a piece of paper and drop it into a large box. A woman's name is drawn. She's then led to the town square, where the entire community stones her to death. The image is too familiar. I cringe, desperate for the class to end. When the bell finally rings, I am nearly sick with relief. As I walk down the hall to gym, Jacklyn and several of her friends stop me by the lockers.

"Want to get high?" Jacklyn asks, a smirk on her face.

"What?" I reply.

"You know, smoke a joint," she answers, stifling a giggle.

"No, thanks," I say, wishing she would just go away.

"Oh, come on, Blanco, don't be such a priss," A.J. chimes in, glancing over at Jacklyn mischievously.

"Okay, fine, let's do it," I demand. "Who's got a match?"

Suddenly, they all burst into laughter. "Right, like any of us would want your disgusting dog lips to touch anything of ours."

"Screw you," I respond.

"What did you say?" A.J. whispers.

"I said, screw you."

"You better watch where you walk, bitch," Jacklyn says icily. "You're dead meat."

Stupid, stupid, stupid! Why did I take their bait? I gave them exactly what they wanted.

Shaken, I go to speech practice. Since the incident with Mr. Horn in the spring, Mrs. Adams's enthusiasm for working with me seems to have dulled. She is just going through the motions of coaching me for this weekend's tournament.

"Jodee, I think you're ready for Saturday. Just do your best," she remarks after only thirty minutes of rehearsal.

"But Mrs. Adams," I reply. "Antigone's monologue is really hard. I'm not confident. Please can we go over it one more time?"

"No, I have an appointment," she announces, putting on her coat. "You'll be fine."

Saturday morning, I awaken with a sense of dread. When Mr. Palmerton coached me for the drama tournament two years ago, I was carefully prepared. I knew exactly what to expect. Mrs. Adams isn't even attending today's competition.

"Come on, angel, time to leave," mom announces cheerfully.

"Mom, I don't want to do this. I have a really bad feeling about it."

"Jodee, you're officially entered. You can't not show up."

"Why not?"

"It's quitting and I won't let you do it. Besides, I'm looking forward to rooting you on!"

Knowing it's pointless to argue, I get in the car. "Mom, this isn't a big deal like the state tournament. It's just a few schools. I'd really rather go on my own. If I win today, you can watch me in the district competitions next month."

"Honey, are you sure?"

"Yeah, mom, I am."

Today's meet is at Anderson, another high school a few miles from Samuels. I walk up to the sign-in desk outside the school's main gym to check in. The paperwork completed, I hand it to the attendant and am given the list of participants competing against me in the category of dramatic interpretation. I shiver when I read it. Dara from Morgan Hills Academy is one of the names.

Memories come flooding back. Dara burning the back of my hand with a lit cigarette . . . she, Kat, Steve, and their friends throwing me in the mud and kicking me as they chanted their hate for me . . . my favorite shoe floating in the toilet . . . my new white sweater, wet and stained, lying on the floor in a puddle of Coke. I begin to shake, terrified of facing Dara. I run into the ladies' room to gather my wits. Taking a deep breath, I walk out to the gym and take my seat next to the other competitors. Dara sees me. She smiles innocently, as if I'm an old friend. I turn my head, wishing I could crawl into bed and stay there.

The minutes pass like hours as I watch the other participants present their monologues. There are twenty of us. Five will be chosen to compete in the district tournament. Finally, my name is called. Dara is still smiling at me, as if nothing ever happened between us. I bet she honestly doesn't remember what she and the others did to me back then. The bullies never remember, but the outcasts never forget. To kids like Dara, it's all just a natural part of growing up. And why shouldn't they feel that way, when that's exactly what they're told by their parents—and even their teachers? The whole thing makes me sick.

I begin my presentation. Dara watches me, her face awash with boredom. *Please God, let me make the finals.*

My monologue over, I take a bow. The applause is reserved. Dara steps up to the podium next. She launches into her monologue, a piece from Arthur Miller's play *The Crucible*. When she finishes, the applause is thunderous. I can feel the rage building inside me. "At least I'll make the finals," I tell myself confidently.

But when I walk over to the board to check the list of finalists, Dara's name and four others are illuminated. Mine is not. I can hear glass shattering in my head. I cover my ears with my hands, hoping to muffle the sound. I run outside, looking for my mom's car. She should be here by now. I feel as if I'm going to explode. I have never experienced anger like this before. It's like Dara is getting rewarded for all her cruelty. All I can think of is killing her and every single person like her who has ever teased and taunted me in school. It's not fair that the one person who nearly destroyed me with cruelty should win at the one thing I've always been good at.

Mom pulls up. I get in the car. My insides are contorted with fury.

"Angel, what is it?"

Calmly, almost too calmly, I relay the events of the morning. Mom grabs my hand and squeezes it. I remain silent the rest of the ride home. When I walk into the house, I go to the kitchen and open the drawer where we keep the butcher knives. I pull out the largest knife. I hold it up in front of the window, watching the light bounce off its gleaming blade.

Mom screams. "Jodee, what are you doing?" she asks, her voice thick with fear.

"I'm going to cut out Dara's heart, and the hearts of everyone else who's hurt me," I reply, trembling. "I want to kill them like they're killing me."

"Angel, please, give me the knife."

"No. They're going to pay."

"Jodee, that's enough. This won't solve anything."

"Fine, have it your way."

I tighten my grip on the knife and begin cutting my face. I am screaming. "Mommy, make it all stop."

Suddenly, I feel strong hands grab my arms. "What in the hell are you doing?" my grandfather yells. The knife drops to the floor. My mom picks it up, puts it in the sink, and closes the knife drawer.

"We better take this kid to the doctor," my grandfather says to my mom.

Slowly, they walk me to the car. We go to the emergency room. I am crying tears of rage. The salt from my tears burns the open cuts on my cheeks. I shudder at the hopelessness of it all. Throughout my entire life, my family, teachers, and doctors keep telling me that one day I'll laugh at all the pain I've suffered. "One day, you'll be on top of the world," they tell me, "and all the kids who were cruel to you will be nowhere. They'll be jealous of you one day. You'll succeed in ways they never will." "He who laughs last, laughs best," daddy has said to me time after time.

They're all lies. If anything they said to me was true, it would have been *me* on that list of finalists today, and not Dara. They lied to me. They all lied.

As murderous images dance across my mind, the E.R. doctor injects me with a tranquilizer. The next thing I know, I'm in my own bed, tucked neatly under the covers, our family dog Shu Shu curled up at my feet. Did I dream today? Or did the things I think I remember really happen? I get a chill when I touch my fingers to my face and feel bandages across my cheeks. Frightened and angry, I do what I always do for solace. I grab my notebook and pen and write a poem.

Reasons

You're prettier than me. You're all prettier than me.
Bang – Bang – You're Dead!
You're smarter than me. You're all smarter than me.
Bang – Bang – You're Dead!
You're better than me. You're all better than me.
Bang – Bang – You're Dead!

Now I'm the prettiest. Now I'm the smartest.
Now I'm the best
Now I'm the loneliest . . .

After the event with the knife, I descend into a severe depression. I stop eating. It's not that I'm trying to starve myself, it's just that food simply won't go down. It sticks in my throat and makes me gag. I am five foot six and my weight has dropped to less than one hundred pounds. To be honest, I am happy about this. Why? Because the problem with my breasts has been getting worse. One breast has grown four times larger than the other, and they have no muscle. They hang limply out of my chest, and the nipples are huge and inverted. I look like a circus freak. Mom and dad have taken me to endocrinologists and other specialists, but they all say the same thing. Corrective surgery can't be performed until I'm seventeen, which is still two more years away. The girls in my gym class will have noticed it way before then. Being emaciated makes my deformity much less obvious. It's turning out to be a perverse solution.

Mom and dad are beside themselves with worry. They keep taking me to doctors and nutritionists. One says I have anorexia, but I don't. I've never seen myself as fat. Food won't go down, period. Another doctor tells us that I have a tumor and that's why my behavior has become so erratic. But when we get a second opinion and additional x-rays are taken, the tumor theory is ruled out. My parents even seek a hypnotist to try to get me to eat. It doesn't work.

By the end of sophomore year, I have no desire to leave

the house anymore. All summer, I lay in my favorite chair in the family room and watch soap operas and reruns of *Bewitched* and *I Dream of Jeannie*. I don't even wish to bathe. I don't want to talk to anyone on the phone. I don't want to see anyone. Paul has come down from college several times to try to snap me out of my sadness. It's too late. It's not that I want to die—I'm not suicidal. If I were, I would have slit my wrists or overdosed on pills a long time ago. I just want to be quiet and left alone. That's all. No big deal. Maybe I'll be lucky. Maybe I'll fall asleep and not ever have to wake up again.

chapter nine

Discovering
Atlantis

It's Friday evening. The weekend spreads out before me like a vast wasteland. I close my eyes to try and shut out the loneliness. I feel like I'm losing my mind. The television is blaring. I hear the weatherman blather on about a tornado warning. He makes a remark about twisters being unusual in Chicago in autumn. "Perhaps it will move toward the lake and become a water spout," he continues. I listen to his chirpy voice, imagining there's someone above him pulling on strings to make him move.

I imagine there's a Muppet meteorologist on *Sesame Street*. Perhaps that's who this weatherman is. I must remember to ask Kermit the Frog about this. Kermit is such an agreeable little guy. He reminds me of Kirby, my favorite Christmas elf. Kirby hates being an elf and dreams only of becoming a dentist. Exiled by the other elves and Santa for being different, he packs his bags and leaves the North Pole. During his travels, he discovers the Land of Misfit Toys, where he meets Rudolph the Red-Nosed Reindeer, the Abominable Snowman, a rubber duck who can't float, a doll with a frown instead of a smile, and a jack-in-the-box with no spring. Like Kirby, they, too, are forgotten outcasts. But things turn out all right for Kirby and his new friends. Rudolph saves them all. Kirby wins back Santa's love and the respect of his elfin brethren and sets up a successful dental practice at the North Pole. The Misfit Toys and the Abominable Snowman find love and acceptance. And everyone lives happily ever after.

"Jodee, why don't you take a shower and get dressed? You need to get out of the house," mom says, interrupting my thoughts. "Throw on a pair of jeans and we'll go to the mall."

"When did you get home? I didn't even hear you come in," I reply, irritated.

"I just got back from the grocery store. Honey, you've got to pull yourself out of this funk."

"It's not a funk, mom. I just don't care about anything anymore. And don't even think about dragging me to another shrink because I won't go."

Mom walks away, frustrated because she loves me dearly and can't help. I feel for her, I do. But something inside me has snapped. I'm turning mean and sour. I didn't ask to be here. She brought me into this world. Now I want out. And screw anyone who needs me to stay. I have heard that some cancer patients have been able to cure themselves by visualizing their healthy cells eating the cancerous ones. I wonder if the opposite would work. There's always hope.

"Jodee, your dad's on the phone," mom yells from the kitchen.

"I don't want to talk to anyone."

"Jodee, he's not anyone, he's your father, and he's calling from Athens. You get up off that chair, young lady, and come over here and talk to him."

Slowly, I uncross my legs, let out an aggravated sigh, and move toward the phone. Mom hands me the receiver.

"Hi, daddy."

"Hello, angel. You know how you've always loved archaeology?" he asks.

"Yeah, why?"

"How would you like to visit the Lost City of Atlantis?"

"What?" I respond.

"There's a volcanic island here called Santorini. Jacques Cousteau believes it may be the fabled Atlantis. You remember daddy's old friend Ernie? Well, he owns a home on Santorini and he's invited us to spend a couple of weeks with him. I've seen this place and I think you and mom will love it. I've bought the airline tickets. You'll leave tomorrow, and we'll go on to Santorini from here."

"What about school? First semester's barely begun, and I've already missed so many days. I was planning on going back Monday."

"Your mother and I have already talked with the principal. He knows your situation. He spoke with your teachers and they've agreed that if you write a ten-page paper about the trip, they'll help you catch up with your studies when we return."

I know I've been a real jerk lately. Maybe going to this island will help all of us. "Okay, daddy, it sounds like fun."

Mom hugs me tightly. We both tell dad we love him and then hang up. "You better start packing," mom says, smiling. Though I've never been to Europe and I'm excited about seeing such a remarkable place, a part of me resists any movement. Going to the airport will mean leaving the house. I hope I can do it.

The next morning, I wake up to the sound of my mom's

voice. "Come on, angel, time to get up."

"Mom, I don't think I want to go to Greece after all."

"Jodee, one of your dreams has always been to see ancient Greece. You've talked about it since you were little. Don't let these kids at school take that away from you. Daddy will be so disappointed if we don't go. All he wants is your happiness. Please, honey, we need this time together."

Within two hours, we are ready to go. As we ride in the cab to O'Hare Airport, I ask my mom to read me the brochure on Santorini. I become engrossed as she describes our destination. For the first time in months, I am encouraged by the promise of tomorrow.

Santorini is the jewel of the Aegean. Thought to be the famed Lost City of Atlantis that Plato wrote about in Critias, *this island offers wonders unlike any others in Europe. Nearly four thousand years ago, a great volcano erupted, splitting this island into five pieces. The largest, Thíra, named after King Thiras, is seventeen miles long by three miles wide and shaped like a crescent moon. Still untouched by commercial development, Santorini is rugged and simple, its luxuries the breathtaking view and the generosity and spirit of the people who live there.*

Travel back in time to the land of the ancients, a magical place where truth and legend become one. Santorini, an adventure of the soul, a memory of a lifetime. ■

Hours later, our airplane lands in Athens, where daddy meets us. The airport is crackling with energy. It reminds me of a flea market on a busy Saturday afternoon, but instead of a mob of bargain hunters, it's a throng of harried travelers searching for their luggage or rushing into the arms of waiting loved ones.

Mom and I don't have an extra moment. Our flight to Santorini departs in forty-five minutes. Clutching our purses and carry-on bags, we hurry through the crowded terminal to our gate. As we near the entrance, my dad comes toward us.

"I was afraid you weren't going to make it," dad says, grabbing our bags and kissing us both.

While we're waiting at the gate, I peer out the window onto the runway. "Dad, where's our jet?" I inquire, confused. "All I see parked out there is that old army plane." I then realize that we're the only people waiting for the flight to Santorini. "Where are the other passengers?"

"There are no other passengers," dad says, grinning. "It's just the three of us and the pilot."

"Tony, you've got to be kidding," mom jumps in.

"Think of this as a family adventure," dad suggests cheerfully.

"Jodee, let it never be said that your mother isn't a good sport!" mom remarks, ducking her head as we board the tiny aircraft, its propellers whirring noisily.

After thirty stomach-lurching minutes in the air, the pilot, who looks like the captain of a fishing boat with his deep tan and faded blue cap, informs us that we are directly above Santorini. I press my face up against the small window. The raw, untamed beauty before me seems artificial, as if I am staring at a postcard. Great, jagged pieces of earth that look as if they were carved from bolts of lightning jut out of the topaz water. I can see the volcano's silent, black mouth. Whitecaps nip at its edges, as if trying to tease it out of its sleep. Inland, herds of goat and sheep graze through open green fields nestled between ancient ruins and mountains the colors of espresso and copper. Where molten lava once burned, life has burst forth out of the fertile ashes. Fruit groves and grape vines stretch on for miles. The power of nature and the spirit of man have collided and coalesced for thousands of years here, making it a hypnotic place.

For such a small aircraft, our landing is surprisingly smooth. "*Kalos irthate*," the pilot says, opening the small door at the front of the plane to let us out.

"What does that mean?" I ask, eager to learn as much Greek as possible in two weeks.

"It means 'welcome,'" he replies.

The airport is a tiny gray structure. Behind it is a turret that reminds me more of Rapunzel's tower than an air-traffic control center. Eager to collect the bags and explore the island, I ask my dad where the luggage ramp is. He smiles and points to a large red wagon sitting in the middle of the runway filled with parcels of mail and boxes. "Our bags are in there," he explains, walking us toward it. "Remember, this is an adventure!"

We carefully begin the task of sorting through dozens of packages. When we locate our suitcases and manage to hoist them out of the wagon, we proceed to the arrival area, which consists of a room with a few metal folding chairs, one desk, and a small stand that sells coffee and home-made cheese pies.

"Antonio, Antonio!" someone shouts from outside. I turn and see a heavy-set fellow with an unruly dark mustache gesturing animatedly at my father. My dad explains that this warm, colorful character is Leftereis, an old friend of Ernie's who is driving us to the house. He then helps my dad load our luggage into his cab and off we go.

We drive along rugged cliffs, past prehistoric caves and colossal rock formations that look like something out of the pages of Jules Verne's *Journey to the Center of the Earth.* We are surrounded by ocean. My ears pop from the altitude as we climb higher into the mountains, then move down through the valley and into the bustling village of Fira. As we wind through rows of whitewashed storefronts, I hear music pouring out of every window and local businessmen shouting and laughing, their deep, robust voices crisscrossing the little town square. *"Adai vrai, katse kala."* I let my senses drink it all in: the smells of lamb rotating on a spit, bread baking in open stone ovens, freshly caught fish being sold on the corner, and wildflowers peeking out of cracks in the stones.

We continue past the main square toward Firostefani, a picturesque hamlet a mile above sea level that's built along the edge of a cliff. We stop in front of a monastery. An old cobblestone donkey path winds from the base of the monastery steps down the side of a steep bluff. In the distance, I can hear the sounds of donkey hooves on the cobblestones and the tinkle of bells from their collars as they trot down toward the old port.

"We go on foot from here," dad informs us. Gulping, mom and I gingerly follow dad and Leftereis. I hear the surf pounding against the rocks below us, and the sound of my gym shoes scuffling across the slippery cobblestones. It is nearly dusk, and the air grows cool. The wind gusts from the north make my nylon jacket flutter. We come to a row of crudely constructed cement steps and a gate. "This is it," dad says, beaming. We descend a steep set of stairs down to a cozy whitewashed structure built into a cave.

We're standing on a large terrace with a panoramic view of all of Santorini. The twinkling lights of Fira cast a pinkish hue on the hundreds of little white houses and round churches with bright blue domes dotting the island's rocky landscape. Beyond the roofs of the buildings are black-sand beaches and acres of vineyards. Directly in front of us, lying dormant in the turquoise water, is the volcano. A flotilla of cruise ships circles it, their foghorns echoing in the distance, warning small fishing vessels of their presence. A mist is rising out of the sea at the caldera's base. If ever there were a place where the spirits of the ancients dance among the living, it is here in this idyllic setting.

"This is a traditional Santorini house, or *spiti*," dad explains. "In 1956, a horrible earthquake destroyed the island. A decade later, an architect restored these homes to their original beauty. Come on, I'm anxious to show you the inside."

There is a living room with a stone couch built into the wall. Farther back is the bedroom, where the bed is also built into the wall. To the right is a tiny alcove with a small refrigerator and an electric burner.

"Where's the bathroom?" mom asks, concerned.

"That's the best part," dad replies. He escorts us back

out onto the terrace and tells us to open the door to our right. Inside are a sink, a shower, and a toilet. A window opens on the ocean side. "I know it's rudimentary," dad says, "but where else in the world can you look at a dazzling view like this while you shampoo your hair?" Dad is so excited to be sharing Santorini with mom and me. For once, it isn't pain or grief bringing us closer, but the joy of discovery.

As we walk down to the village for dinner, we watch the setting sun. It's a spectacular sight. As it sets, the sky is illuminated in velvety hues of fuchsia, orange, and purple. A chorus of sounds accentuates the moment, the clicking of donkey hooves, the chiming of church bells, and the faint chugging of a moped as it struggles up a hill.

There are only three restaurants on the entire island: This place is simple and unspoiled. There are no malls or movie theaters. There isn't even a grocery store. If you want fruit, you go to the *manavi*, a person who sells produce in the village square. Meat is available only through a butcher shop. And cheese is bought from a local dairy. If you're hungry for fish, you can ride a mule to the old port, where you will be met by local fishermen who will hand you a bucket and instruct you to choose your *psari* right out of the net.

This magical island releases me somehow. I am free and exuberant. School seems far away; another world. Mom keeps reminding me that we'll have to go back to reality in ten days. But now, Santorini is my reality. Why is it that people always identify reality with unhappiness, as if everyone is supposed to be miserable, and if they're not, it can't be real life?

How I'm dreading junior year. It's the sex year—all the cool girls lose their virginity by then. At the very least, they're getting into heavy petting. What am I going to do? My breasts are so deformed that if a boy saw them, he'd be repulsed. And if I neck with someone, he'll think I'm a prude if I don't let him go to the next base. Either way, I face rejection.

Here in Santorini, that would never be an issue. This is a conservative place. "Good girls" don't go out with boys unless they're accompanied by a parent or guardian. Boys would never think of trying to cop a feel with their girl-friends, at least not until they were engaged. Santorini is a different world, and a better one, I believe.

"Honey, does that sound good?" dad asks.

"What? Oh, I'm sorry, daddy, I was daydreaming. What were you saying?"

"I was asking if you'd like to stop here for dinner."

We are standing in front of an adorable little restaurant overlooking the sea. A white sign with blue Greek letters hangs from a blue-and-white awning. The interior is cozy, with only four tables. Outside on the terrace there are six tables. There are blue-and-white checkered tablecloths and a candle on each table. Dad says this is typical. The owner, Yorgos Rousso, an older man with a broad smile and a mane of hair that's so gray it almost looks blue, comes out to greet us with his son, Vangelie, a handsome boy in his early teens. "You must be Ernie's friend Tony," Yorgos says in heavily accented English. "Welcome to Santorini."

"Thank you," dad replies. After warm introductions, my

parents and I sit at one of the tables on the terrace. Dad orders a bottle of local wine for he and mom and a 7-Up for me. When Vangelie returns with our drinks, I ask him for a menu. He smiles and says that restaurants don't have menus in Santorini. You go into the kitchen to see what's being cooked fresh that evening. "The big restaurants have display . . . what is word?" Vangelie asks.

"Cases," I reply. "I think you mean display cases."

"Yes, that is the word. The big restaurants have their dishes in display cases. We are small family place. You come to the kitchen and my mother will show you what we have for tonight."

Dad, mom, and I follow Vangelie into a tiny alcove at the back of the restaurant. It's so small that we go in one at a time. Mrs. Rousso greets us warmly. She doesn't speak any English, so I use the Greek words I've learned today to say, "Hello, it's good to meet you."

"Vangelie, why don't you choose our meals this evening?" dad suggests. "We want a traditional Santorini dinner."

"I happy to," Vangelie responds proudly.

Within minutes, he's back with the first plates of goodies. "These are *domata keftedes*," he explains, pointing to the fragrant golden-brown fritters. Smells of dill and onion waft across the table. "In English, you would call tomato balls and are only made in Santorini," he explains. My parents watch, their relief apparent, as I devour three of the *keftedes*. Next, Vangelie brings out a bowl of something that looks like tan peanut butter. It has bits of garlic sprinkled on the top, and is served with chunks of bread that Mrs.

Rousso just took out of the oven.

"What is this?" I inquire, not sure how I feel about trying it. It's not nearly as appetizing as the fritters.

"Oh, you must to try," Vangelie says. "This is *fava*. I think you call them chicken peas," he explains.

"Chickpeas," dad says.

"We grow them here. They are smaller than your chickpeas, and much more flavors-full. We grind and mix with special spices," he continues. "Put on bread and try, please."

Within minutes, I have eaten four pieces of bread with *fava*. Though it doesn't look so great, it is absolutely delicious. Vangelie continues presenting one sumptuous dish after another, until we can barely lift our forks. This is the first time in as long as I can remember that I have felt full from food, rather than feeling full of sadness.

"One last treat to try," Vangelie says, handing us each a small plate of yogurt with honey. "Greek yogurt very special. The honey comes from our own farm." I dip my spoon into the creamy white substance and bring it to my lips. It tastes rich and sweet. I close my eyes and imagine that I am the Goddess Aphrodite eating my dessert. After dad pays the check and we thank the Roussos for their kindness, mom suggests we walk around Fira for a bit before we go back to the house.

As we make our way toward the town square, I can hear pulsating rock-and-roll music. Down the street on my right, I spot a sign in English that reads "Neptune Discoteque."

"Let's take a peek," dad says. We walk through a long courtyard lined with flowers and pottery and enter a gigantic natural cavern. Stalactites hang above us like mammoth petrified teardrops. Large fishing nets are strewn across the ceiling, and scenes from the ocean are hand-painted on the walls. To our left is a stone bar, where a D.J. is spinning records on an old stereo system. At the other end of the bar, two gorgeous men are making drinks. Behind them, shelves that have been cut into the walls are filled with liquor bottles of every color and size, from Jim Beam and Jack Daniels to Greek ouzo and French brandy. Spread out in front of us are dozens of handcrafted stone tables and benches. Flickering candles adorn each table. In the back of the cave is a dance floor made of solid marble.

We sit at one of the couches. A bartender comes over to our table. He is even better looking up close. I almost can't speak when he asks what I would like to drink. Dad has given me permission to try the local wine, so I ask him for a glass. Mom and dad order the same. "My name is Yianne," he says. "I own this disco."

"*Yia sou*," I reply, my heart skipping a beat. He chats with my family for a moment before returning to the bar. As I look around, I see that there are about twenty customers, all of whom are sexy young guys my age. Soon, one of them approaches and sits next to us. My parents look at me and smile. Mom and I begin to talk with him. He speaks almost no English but we manage to communicate. He explains that his name is Yorgos, that he is seventeen years old and a fisherman's apprentice, and would love to meet me here tomorrow night for a date. My dad, using all of his talent at charades, explains to Yorgos that he and mom will drop me off 8:00 tomorrow evening, and return to pick me up at 11:00. I'm thrilled!

The next day I buy an English/Greek Berlitz phrase book. From that night on, I meet Yorgos and his friends every evening at the disco. We dance to disco and rock-and-roll until ten o'clock every night, and then we do an hour of dancing to traditional Greek *bouzouki*. During the day, we hang out at the beach or visit the ruins. My Greek vocabulary increases by twenty to thirty words a day. Though I have only been on this island a short while, I feel more a part of this place than I have ever felt in the States. I'm accepted and appreciated by my friends here. I always knew there was a larger world than my Midwestern high school, but until now, I wasn't sure if it was a world for me.

In addition to Yorgos and his group, I have also met someone who I know will be a friend forever. His name is Niko. Strong and handsome with dark eyes and a creative passion, he is an enigma on this tiny island, where almost everyone is native Santorinian. Born and raised in the city of Salonika in northern Greece, Niko has an avant-garde style that most of the people who live here don't understand. He's moved here to open a nightclub in Fira that he's going to call Casablanca. Niko and I are kindred spirits. He doesn't follow the crowd either. I think that's why he's building a club inspired by the one in the movie. I think he identifies with Bogart's character.

Niko and I spend a lot of time together talking about what it's like to be different. He's the first person I've ever met who can genuinely empathize with the pain I've experienced. One afternoon, we're sitting in the bar of his empty club, sharing bitter experiences from our childhood. Casually, he asks me, "Why is such a pretty girl like you so lonely?" I decide to take a giant leap and tell him about my deformity. Deep down, I'm terrified, but I know that if we're going to have the genuine friendship I suspect we will, I have to level with him here and now. I'm so tired of keeping my body a secret from others. Tentatively, I say, "Niko, the reason my parents brought me to Santorini was to get my mind off wanting to die. The kids back home hate me because I'm different. On top of that, I'm a freak. My breasts aren't growing normally. The doctors say I'll need surgery in a couple of years."

He looks straight into my eyes and says, "*Agapi mou*, my love, you must never be ashamed of any part of yourself." Then, he gently asks, "Is it all right if I look at the beauty that you believe is ugly?" Though numb with fear, something inside me trusts him and I know I must say yes. With trembling fingers, I unbutton my blouse. I'm self-conscious about my bra, which is more of a contraption than a garment of clothing, with its labyrinth of belts, buckles, and straps. He sees me fumbling to unhook it and says reassuringly, "Don't be afraid, nothing you can show me will make me stop being your friend." Finally, the loosened bra falls to my waist and I am standing there, my hideousness in plain view. He smiles, and then to my utter surprise, says, "*Pou einai to problema*. Where's the problem?"

"Are you blind? Look at me!" I cry.

"I am looking at you, and I think you're beautiful, and one day, a husband will, too," he responds.

When I look at Niko, I know that as long as I have his friendship and the wonders of this island, I can survive anything. In the States, everyone sees me as the misfit. In Santorini, I'm the belle of the ball. I feel like Cinderella. My high school is just the evil stepmother's basement, and Santorini is the prince's grand palace where anything is possible. Ten thousand miles away, in an exotic, foreign land, I have discovered the simple joys of being a normal, happy American teenager. Whenever things get too tough for me at Samuels, I'm going to close my eyes and imagine that I am back here, sipping Greek coffee with Niko, or dancing at Neptune's.

This trip has changed my family's life. No longer tense and worried, we can laugh again. There is no more talk of me being a social failure; no more arguments over who's at fault. It's as if the bad memories have evaporated.

When we get back to the States, I am determined to learn Greek. My mom takes me to a Hellenic church near our house. I ask the priest, Father Byron, an avuncular personality in his late fifties, to recommend a Greek teacher. He doesn't believe I am serious because "No one, unless they have Greek roots, can learn the language."

"Father," I reply, "I'm your first exception."

He introduces me to the strictest teacher I've ever had. A beautiful woman in her mid-thirties, Heleni is serious about education. She has never accepted a non-Greek student before. "Jodee, I'll teach you only if you remain dedicated. If your homework isn't done or you're not prepared more than twice in a row, I will stop your lessons," she warns.

"I promise, Heleni. I won't let you down. This means so much to me."

Satisfied I'm sincere, she starts tutoring me for ninety minutes twice a week. When she begins to address me in the familiar tense, I know I've passed the test.

chapter ten

Freak

Show

I've only been back from Santorini for a month and already it's started. Despite trying to stay positive, to hold on to my memories of my friends in Greece and the times we shared together, I wake up every morning with a gnawing anxiety. I never know what looms ahead once I leave the house. When my alarm clock sounds, I hide under the covers, fold my hands, and pray that I am suddenly stricken with mono or strep throat—anything contagious that will prevent me from going to school.

I have gained back all the weight I lost. My parents are relieved but I'm desperate. The added pounds accentuate the abnormality of my breasts. My right breast is huge and disfigured. It resembles an engorged water balloon. My left breast is worse—it is one-fifth the size of the right one, and it has no flesh or muscle. It looks like an arthritic knuckle sticking out from under my skin. As I stare in the mirror trying to decide which blouse offers the best camouflage, I am ashamed. In the past when other kids called me a freak, I could tell myself that they were wrong. Now, as I struggle to hook the bra that has to be specially made to accommodate my deformity, I am not so sure. The bra is padded on one side and looks peculiar. It is clumsy and full of strange straps and buckles to compensate for the weight one side has to support.

I remember when my mom and I went to buy it. This old woman with large scaly hands kept poking and prodding me with a yellow tape measure. I felt like a thing instead of a girl.

I keep asking myself, "Why did this happen to my body?" My classmates have yet another reason to justify hurting me. I dread walking through the halls at Samuels and having to endure the even greater threats and taunting. I know if I want to change schools, my parents will let me, but that would just be running away.

I've withstood pain and loneliness since the fifth grade. I only have two more years of high school left. If I transfer now, it's a tacit surrender. I can't let my classmates defeat me like that. I can survive this. If anyone had told me what I was walking into, I would have grabbed one of my grandfather's antique razors and used it to quiet the suffering once and for all.

As I lay in bed, my mind spinning, my mom comes in, full of exaggerated cheer. I love her for trying to infuse me with her optimism, but on mornings like this, it drives me nuts. "Mom, you're such a Pollyanna," I declare. "You think just because I'm back to a healthy weight that anything will be different? What about my ugly chest? I wish I could take a knife and cut these hideous tits right off." Mom means well, but nothing she can say is going to elevate my mood.

"Daddy and I can put you in another school," she says hopefully. "You were so happy on our trip to Santorini, and I don't want you to be dragged back down again."

"Mom, you don't understand. It doesn't matter where I go to school. We've tried that before. It's always the same thing. I'll just tough it out."

"Remember, angel, you can rise above all this. Don't give those kids the satisfaction of knowing they hurt you. Just ignore them and walk away."

Yeah, right.

I finally choose an off-white angora sweater, my favorite jeans, and a pair of cowboy boots. This particular sweater hides my problem well. I just have to make sure it doesn't get wet. In Illinois, gym is required unless you bring a letter from a doctor. My parents think it's better for my pediatrician to cite another medical reason when he requests that I be excused from gym. They're concerned that I'll be embarrassed and self-conscious if my teachers know the truth. So Dr. Kalen writes that I have a back problem that can be exacerbated by strenuous movement. Lying to my teachers proves to be a serious mistake.

When I hand Dr. Kalen's note to my gym instructor, Ms. Nichols, she immediately scoffs. A tough, no-nonsense woman who looks more like a drill sergeant than a girl's basketball coach, she thinks it's ridiculous that I should be excused from her physical ed class just because of a sore back.

"That's what's wrong with parents and pediatricians, today," she comments, folding the piece of paper and shoving it into her pocket. "They're overprotective. You can't be too soft on kids or we'll end up with a society of wimps and prisses."

"Ms. Nichols, you can talk with Dr. Kalen. Believe me, it's no fun to be the one who sticks out. I would much rather join in like everybody else, but I can't."

"All right," she says resignedly. "Bring your books with you so you can use the hour productively."

"Thanks, Ms. Nichols."

Every afternoon is the same, for weeks and weeks. I go to gym, and while the other girls practice volleyball, I sit on the floor with my books spread out in front of me. Pretending to study, I write poem after poem, spilling my frustration and sadness onto the pages of a spiral-bound notepad.

There are times I become so immersed in my writing that I'm able to block out the ribbing from my classmates. Still, they are relentless.

"Miss Priss, you suck."

"No wonder you like hanging out with the retards, you spaz, you cripple."

"Why don't you take gym—you have cooties or something?"

After several weeks, I ask Ms. Nichols if she'll give me a library pass. I explain to her that it's uncomfortable for me to sit by the bleachers while everyone else is participating in gym. "Jodee, life isn't always comfortable. It's time everyone stops babying you. I'm sorry, but the answer is no. Believe me, you'll thank me for this one day." If Ms. Nichols and the other teachers were aware of what was *really* going on, that I'm disfigured and waiting to be approved for radical recon-structive surgery, they might be more understanding. Instead, their disdain sets the tone for the students.

Between classes, some of the kids gather in groups as I'm walking down the hall. They hunch over in hideous poses, distort their faces, and pretend to be spastic. Grunting and flailing their arms, they chase me until they get bored, at which point they explode into giggles and walk away. I am growing so tired of the teasing. I watch couples kissing in the schoolyard or in the halls and the cheerleaders in their short skirts and tight sweaters smiling and laughing, sharing secrets, exchanging makeup. What I wouldn't give for just one day of what they have . . .

I imagine a Faustian bargain with the popular students at school. They'll treat me as if I'm their favorite person for one day. The quarterback of the football team will be my boyfriend and walk me to class, holding my hand. The cheerleaders will look up to me, and argue amongst themselves about which of them is my best friend. All the cool people will race to share their secrets with me, and I'll be the first person to be invited to the big party on Saturday night. In exchange, after my twenty-four hours are up, I let them do anything they want to me: beat me, spit at me, call me names, even see my deformity. I would pay that price just to know the ecstasy of being liked and accepted for a single day.

How I wish I could twitch my nose like Samantha on *Bewitched* and transport myself to Santorini. Every week, I receive letters from my friends on the island. It's fun translating them with Heleni. Those letters make life more bearable, but they also make me miss my friends there even more.

The situation with gym is becoming intolerable. Word has spread that there's something wrong with me, and my classmates mock me incessantly. I also am starting to hurt physically. The condition with my breasts creates severe pain because of the abnormal weight on only one side. The tissue is growing faster than the muscle, which puts pressure on the nerves in the area. Sometimes, it feels like the inside of my breast is being poked with a hot wire. On this particular day, the pain is so intense, I think I might vomit. I go to the nurses' office to lie down until the worst of it passes. As I'm leaving, Jacklyn and A.J., both of whom are in my gym class, smile and start a normal conversation with me. Jacklyn is chomping on a piece of bubblegum so large that she is almost unintelligible. I should be suspicious, but I am still in considerable pain and not thinking straight. It all happens so fast that I don't have time to respond.

A.J. suddenly grabs my wrist, holding it tightly so I can't move. Jacklyn, emphasizing every gesture, places her perfectly manicured fingers inside her mouth and extracts this massive wad of pink chewing gum the size of a golf ball, stretching and pulling on it. Next, A.J. holds me down while Jacklyn works the gum deep into my hair, tangling it so badly that later, the school nurse has to cut out the sticky mass with scissors.

What's left of my hair is beyond embarrassing. I have great chunks missing near the nape of the neck and toward the top of my scalp. I consider a wig, but the idea seems too weird. When I get home and mom sees my hair, she tries to convince me once again to transfer to another school.

"Forget it, mom, the answer is no. I won't run away."

"Okay, angel," she responds. "I respect your decision."

She and Aunt Evie take me to the beauty shop where my hair is cut and restyled. I have to admit, it looks better, but nothing escapes the shrewd eyes of teenagers. The next day, my hair becomes the focus of their fun. They don't really say anything, they just follow me into the bathroom or down the halls, stare right at my hair, then burst into laughter. I want to crawl in a hole. I feel ugly and dirty, as if my breasts—and now my hair—are grime that I need to scrub off with soap and water.

When I get home after school, mom and I quarrel. I'm frustrated and tired as hell of being told to "rise above it all." What I really want to do is kick some ass. "Show them how strong you are by ignoring them," mom insists.

Why must mom continue pushing her grown-up logic on me? Kids simply don't think that way. Adults perceive the act of ignoring someone as a sign of power. Teenagers think it spells weakness with a capital *W*. The more I pretend indifference, the harder my classmates try to get my goat. Mom just doesn't get it: Teens are different than adults. I care about my mom's opinion of me, and it's really causing a predicament. Instead of fighting back at school, which is what I should do, I try to act mature and walk away because I don't want my mom to be disappointed in me. But what about my own sense of self? Mom is so worried about my dignity that she never stops to consider my pride.

"Mom, you'll never understand what I'm going through. You talk as if I live in a plastic bubble where everybody behaves like an adult," I say, exasperated. "Why can't I just move to Santorini? I hate it here." Mom's eyes well with tears.

"Mom, I'm sorry," I reply, giving her a hug.

"I'm sorry, too, angel," she responds, squeezing me tightly. "At least we talk. I'd much rather you get this off your chest." The unintended pun makes us both laugh. Then we have a good cry and eat my grandmother's macaroni and cheese. As we devour our favorite food, I can't help but worry that mom still doesn't understand the severity of what I'm facing at school: Ignoring these kids only makes them more determined. You'd think she and dad would have a different perspective on things in light of all that happened in junior high, but they still hold to their belief that turning your back on bullies is the only way to deal with them.

The next morning, I make an important decision. I tell my parents that I am going to start gym again. "Honey," mom says, "if you take gym, you'll have to shower with the other girls. How are you going to prevent them from seeing your problem?"

"I'll undress really fast and get in and out of the shower before anyone sees me."

I have to do something, and this seems to be the best solution. On the school bus, I say a prayer. *Please, God, don't let anyone see what I really look like.*

All day, I keep reminding myself to be brave. Later that morning, I bump into Noreen in the hall. She smiles weakly and says hello, but her face is shrouded in sadness. All the years of teasing and taunting have taken a tremendous toll on her. I still have some fight left in me, while she's become a shell of who she once was. Now when we see each other, it's no longer warm and friendly, but rather, strained and uncomfortable. Pain is a tenuous bond. Like so many outcasts, our relationship wasn't built on the positive qualities we had in common, but on the terrible suffering we shared. We've become like prisoners of war. The difference between our outlooks is that I continue to have hope that we'll be freed.

Soon, it's the afternoon, and I am walking through the door to the girls' locker room. It feels as though there are weights on my feet. I have brought along a box of tampons as my prop. As everyone around me begins to undress for gym, I make an obvious gesture of pulling a tampon out of my bag, making sure that the girls right next to me see it. I then grab my uniform, run to the bathroom behind the lockers, and change inside one of the stalls. No one thinks anything of it, since it isn't unusual for a girl to want privacy if she is having her period. The tampon trick also gets me out of having to take a shower, because the health code forbids use of the showers if you are menstruating.

My ruse works for the first few weeks, until Sharon approaches me near the sink. "Why don't you change out here with the rest of us? You have a disease or something?" she asks. What is it about Sharon and me and bathrooms? I recall the two of us standing in the girls' lavatory freshman year and me wiggling out of her invitation to smoke by saying that I had a cold and didn't want her to catch it. I pulled one over on her then, but it appears that I'm not going to be that lucky this time.

"Leave me alone," I reply, my eyes scanning the immediate vicinity in search of the easiest escape. I could shove her, but that will only give her an excuse to hit me. If I make a dash for the door, everyone will call me a chicken. The nervousness in my voice fuels her enjoyment.

"What are you looking for? You think someone's gonna help you? We all hate you," Sharon says, fixing me with a menacing stare. I'm beginning to understand what it must feel like to be attacked in the tabloids. It doesn't matter what you have or haven't done. All that counts is what's being said about you.

Suddenly, Ms. Nichols enters the locker room. *Thank God.* "Sharon, why aren't you changed for gym yet? Is there a problem?"

"No, Ms. Nichols. I was just asking Jodee if she had an extra tampon," Sharon answers innocently.

"Well, hurry up," Ms. Nichols says, exiting.

"You're such a weirdo," Sharon remarks. "So many people at this school want to kick the daylights out of you. If I were you, I'd be careful where I go." Satisfied that she's got me good and scared, she turns and walks away.

If my classmates see my chest, I'll get crucified. There's only one solution: speed. I have math right before gym. Every day I watch the clock and listen for the bell. The second it rings, I leap out of my desk and run: The campus is nearly two city blocks long. My math class is at one end, and the gym at the other. I have less than five minutes to make it to the locker room and change before anyone else arrives. As soon as gym is over, I rush to the showers and dart through as quickly as possible. While the other girls are washing and conditioning their hair, I am already dressed with no one the wiser.

But one morning, I'm not fast enough. Sharon catches a glimpse of my breasts before I have a chance to cover them. She bursts out laughing and calls me a freak. She says that no one will ever want to love or marry me, and that I will die a lonely virgin. "You're God's worst mistake," she sings.

Jacklyn and A.J. immediately chime in. "You better run

home to mommy," A.J. hisses. "If we ever catch you alone, we'll beat those ugly tits black and blue." The entourage chuckles, relishing my fear and discomfort. Sharon runs over to my locker. She carefully lifts my bra off the hook, dangling it menacingly in the air. All the girls snicker when they see what my bra looks like. Sharon whips it across the room to Jacklyn, who catches it and tosses it to A.J. Soon, everyone joins in the game, throwing my bra around the locker room like a ball. After each of them has had her fun with it, they throw it in the toilet, along with my silk blouse, then run out the door, giggling.

I am humiliated. I have to go to class to show them that they haven't defeated me. With nothing else to wear, I put the top from my gym uniform on. Because I don't have my special bra, you can see my disfigured breasts through the outline of the cheap cotton shirt. I grab my bookbag and hold it in front of my chest, hoping no one will notice.

When I walk out of the locker room, boys from the football team, some of the wrestlers, and several of the girls from gym class are standing outside waiting for me. I am terrified. "Why is God punishing me like this?" my mind cries out. The malevolence in their eyes is palpable.

I can't run because they have me surrounded. If I scream and get a teacher's attention, I could get them into trouble. I have to make a choice. I either let them degrade me now and get it over with, or attempt rescue from a teacher and be tortured later for being a snitch. "Come on, you guys, please let me go to class," I plead. For a brief moment, I see guilt flicker across several faces, but I know no one will risk going against the pack. They encircle me and the chants begin . . .

"You're an ugly dog."

"Hey, guys, who wants to take the mutant to prom?"

"My dog is even prettier than you, bitch."

"If I suck your tit, will I turn into a toad?"

The verbal assault is relentless. I try to cover my ears, but nothing can drown out the sound of their voices. Then, I see Tyler out of the corner of my eye walking toward the group. Even though he's been a bit of a jerk to me, I still have a crush on him. "Maybe he'll stick up for me," I tell myself hopefully.

"Hey, Blanco," he says, grinning. "Have you ever made out? Right, like anyone would want to touch something like you." Peals of fresh laughter rip through the hallway. With that, they all happily scurry off to their next class.

It feels as if I am falling through a tunnel and all I can hear is the echo of my own voice repeating the words *please stop laughing*. Numb, I sink to the floor and close my eyes. Hugging myself as hard as I can, I begin rocking slowly back and forth, pretending that I am in Santorini and Niko is holding me.

Slowly, I straighten up, gather my books, and go to my next class. When I get home from school, my parents ask me if anything is wrong. I can't bear for them to start worrying about me again. I lie and tell them everything is fine.

The gold-and-russet autumn landscape is turning a wintry gray. This year, it seems that the change in seasons is a reflection of what's happening to me: A cold dampness is setting in. It's not helping that the holidays are just around the corner, either. All I hear as I walk through the halls at school are snippets of conversations about Christmas parties and romantic plans for New Year's Eve. My classmates are all focused on the gifts they're going to buy and the kisses they'll receive underneath the mistletoe.

Since the incident after gym, my classmates have decided they won't allow a "freak" like me to eat in their lunchroom. When they see me at the soda machines, they threaten to beat me. They have made me so scared that I start stuffing my bookbag with breakfast bars and protein snacks each morning before school. Then, at lunchtime, I sneak into the girls' bathroom, sit on the sink, and wolf them down. I have nowhere else to go. Students aren't allowed to leave the school grounds for lunch and eating isn't permitted in class.

One afternoon, Ms. Linstrom, the school librarian and a sweet older woman, finds me in the lavatory. She wraps her arms around me. She gives me a pass for the rest of the semester so that I can have my lunch in the library with her. I confide in Ms. Linstrom the agony I'm going through. She tells me that my classmates are tough on me not because they hate me, but because they don't understand me. "One day your life will change and you'll have so many friends . . . people with whom you have something in common," she says reassuringly.

I love spending time in the library with Ms. Linstrom. It's safe; no one can hurt me there. I read biographies about famous living people and vow that one day I will be part of their lives. Ms. Linstrom also encourages me to write and has entered me in a poetry competition. If I win, I will be given a scholarship to a two-week summer writing and acting workshop at Eastern Illinois University. I cross my fingers.

I manage to keep my spirits up by concentrating on Santorini. Yorgos and his friends send me letters every week and Niko and I talk on the phone often. I'm proud of myself for learning such a difficult language. My dad's proud of me too—he promises that if I keep my grades up and continue progressing with my second language, he'll let me use one of his company cars.

In the interim, I still ride the bus to and from school. The kids are relentless in making fun of my deformity, which is still hot gossip. Every day is a new adventure in humiliation. Almost every afternoon, it's the same routine. I get off the bus, someone knocks me down, grabs my books, and throws them into the middle of the street. I watch while cars run over my books and papers. When there's a break in traffic, I rush out and quickly gather the scattered remnants. One day, I lose my temper. As two of the kids begin shoving and pushing me, I scream "Screw you!" as loudly as I can. They only laugh. The next thing I know, they are grabbing my shoulders and pretending they're going to push me into the street. They are stronger than they think—they push me into traffic and two cars came to a screeching halt just feet away. I never take the bus again. My grandfather, who saw what happened from the window, begins driving me to school every morning and picking me up each afternoon. Though the circumstances that force us together are unfortunate, the time I spend with him is priceless.

With each passing day, I can feel my resolve slipping away. Christmas has me down and out. Mom senses something, but isn't pushing me to open up. I guess she figures I'll talk about it when I'm ready. Instead, she busies herself preparing for Christmas. My parents love the holidays. The interior of our home looks like the display window at Marshall Field's. Each member of our family has an assignment in the decorating process. Mom and dad are in charge of the tree; grandmother is responsible for wrapping garland and strings of lights around all the picture frames, mirrors, and railings in the house; and my grandfather and I do the elves, my favorite part.

Years ago, the company that makes Joy Dishwashing Liquid did a special holiday promotion. For every bottle you purchased, you received a felt Christmas elf. My mom fell in love with these little, smiling figurines, and she must have collected fifty. Grandfather and I spent hours finding just the right places to put them. It was like a treasure hunt. We perched them on lampshades and nestled them among the leaves of my mom's indoor plants. We even had them peeking out of the medicine cabinets in the bathrooms.

Despite all the extravagant decorations, Christmas is subdued. My grandparents, aunts, mom, dad, and I have a traditional ham dinner and exchange gifts. Though I make a grand show of it for my family, ripping the wrapping paper off my presents and diving into the boxes, my mind is somewhere else. I envision Jacklyn and her boyfriend nuzzling each other by a cozy fire; Tyler and his girl drinking eggnog with their friends. I fight back tears.

"Jodee, why don't you sing us a Christmas carol?" dad suggests.

The last thing I want to do is burst into song. But I love my dad and want to make him happy. I belt out "O Holy Night." Everyone claps as I smile and sit down. Shu Shu, our poodle, jumps into my lap, wagging her tail so furiously that it creates a breeze. As I pet her fluffy black ears, I try to imagine what Christmas will be like for me a decade from now. Will I have a career? Will I be married? Will my family be okay? I wish the universe would rush the passage of time so that years would turn into months, and days would become hours. I realize it's probably a sin to think like this, but I want my teen years to finish. If they don't end soon, I fear they may finish *me*.

By the time school reconvenes after Christmas break, I am out of optimism. The loneliness is unbearable. My parents aren't stupid—they see my disposition deteriorating. I finally decide to tell them what's been happening these last few months.

"Are you sure you won't consider transferring to another high school?" dad asks. "At least think about it for next year."

"Okay, daddy. I will."

The next few weeks move at a snail's pace. The teasing at school has grown so intense that I'm exhausted by the end of each day. I still have one more year before I can have plastic surgery to fix my breasts. The surgeons keep telling us the same thing: "Not until she's at least seventeen." My chest hurts so much I can't sleep on my stomach. My doctor has offered to prescribe painkillers, but I don't want any part of them. The last time a specialist gave me pills, I practically turned into a zombie. I'd rather hurt than be spaced out.

Mom continues to be encouraging. Though I usually find her optimism irritating, today it proves prophetic. As I'm walking out of gym, one of the girls from my English class stops me in the hall. Tall with short red hair and a tomboyish exterior, Annie is considered a loner. Because she is always dressed in tight jeans and a black leather jacket, no one ever messes with her. Even Sharon and her crowd are intimidated by Annie's toughness. I can't imagine what she wants to talk to me about.

"Hey, Jodee, I'm having a couple of friends over Friday night, and I was wondering if you wanted to join us," Annie says.

"Are you serious?" I ask, dumbstruck.

"Yeah, why wouldn't I be?" she answers.

"It's just that the few times I've been invited to anything, it's always turned out to be a mean joke," I reply.

"I think it's really cool how you hold your head up despite how bad everyone treats you. You've got a lot of guts. You should forget about these assholes at Samuels and get to know my friends. They'd like you."

"Okay. For sure, I'll come," I respond. We exchange phone numbers and addresses. Friday after school, I can barely contain my excitement. "Mom, what should I wear tonight?" I ask.

"Honey, put on whatever makes you feel the prettiest," my mom advises.

I choose an off-white silk blouse and my lavender Gloria Vanderbilt jeans. I dab a tiny bit of lilac perfume on my wrists. "It's getting late," mom says. "Coming," I respond. Within minutes, we are on our way to Annie's. Her parents have offered to let me spend the night. As we pull into her driveway, Annie and her mom come out to greet us.

"Mrs. Blanco, it's nice to meet you," Annie says. "This is my mom, Virginia." It's hard for me to believe this sweet, caring girl who's treating my mom with such respect is the same person feared by half of Samuels.

"It's so good to meet you both," mom responds. "Jodee has really been looking forward to this evening."

"Annie, too," Virginia says. "Oh, to be that age again."

They chat for a few moments, then my mom leaves.

"Your mom's really cool," Annie remarks as we go into the house.

"Thanks," I reply.

"We'll hang out downstairs," Annie says. "My friends should be here soon."

I follow Annie down a short flight of steps to a large rec room. At the far end is a small round table with platters of hot and cold food and a cooler with cans of soda on ice.

"Who do you want to listen to?" she asks, turning on the stereo. "I've got Rush, Journey, Led Zeppelin . . . "

"Journey," I reply. The rich voice of lead singer Steven Perry fills the room.

"I love this song," Annie comments.

"Yeah, me too," I agree. "Can I ask you something?"

"Sure, shoot."

"You pretend to be so tough at school. But you're really not like that at all. Why the act?"

"Don't be fooled. I'm no angel. I like it that the 'popular' girls are afraid of me. I used to be made fun of, same as you," Annie recalls. "Then I got smart. I figured if I looked tough, I'd be left alone. I was right. I don't think a person needs to be mean to be feared. The girls at school see the chain hanging from my belt buckle and my tattoos, and they're scared to death, but I've never teased a single person at Samuels. I wouldn't do it because I know what that feels like and it's the worst feeling on earth."

As we're talking, two young men arrive who appear to be about nineteen or twenty years old. Annie makes the introductions. "Jodee, this is Bill and Dino. Guys, meet Jodee."

Bill is tall and gangly. His blond hair is cut close to his head. Clad in ripped faded jeans, a Ted Nugent T-shirt, and black army boots, he reminds me of a character out of a 1960s biker movie. He can't stand still—he's constantly shifting his weight from one foot to the other.

Heavyset with a kind smile and curly black hair, Dino looks like Winnie the Pooh in Harley Davidson garb. His calm demeanor is a stark contrast to Bill's frenetic energy.

They both say, "Hello."

"Want a cigarette?" Bill asks, pulling a pack of Marlboros out of his pocket and offering one to me.

"No, thanks," I respond.

"You don't smoke. That's cool. I wish I could quit," he says, turning and walking toward the buffet table.

"He seems like a really nice guy," I remark.

"He gets into trouble sometimes," Annie says. "But he's such a good person. He's always there when I need him."

"Does he live at home?"

"No, that's the problem," Dino says. "His parents are

super-strict. It doesn't help that he's adopted, either. He got so tired of them constantly trying to control him that he finally just packed up and left."

"God, that's awful."

"Yeah," Dino agrees. "I feel bad for him. He lives in this tiny studio apartment and he's always struggling to make his rent."

"What does he do?"

"Whatever he can. Odd jobs. He sells a little weed here and there. Don't say anything to my mom. She likes Bill but she worries he's a 'bad influence' on me. She'd flip out if she knew about the pot thing."

"Everybody, look who's here," Bill shouts.

"Didn't anyone ever tell you not to talk with your mouth full?" says the handsome guy coming down the stairs.

"Who's that?" I ask.

"My brother, David," Annie replies, watching me scope him out. "Boy, are you barking up the wrong tree," she says.

"What do you mean?" I ask.

"What she means is that I'm gay," David answers.

"You're kidding!"

"Nope, but if I were straight, I'd be after you in a flash," he says, walking toward us.

"Thanks," I reply, smiling.

The rest of the evening, the five of us talk. We discuss everything from drugs, dating, and sex to movies and music. We share stories about our past, and the rejection we've suffered. I am beginning to see that the *cool crowd* at Samuels plays in a very small sandbox. Annie's friends operate on a much larger playing field. They're out in the world in a way that most high school kids aren't. Something about how they carry themselves and the way they talk makes me think of the tragic heroes of ancient Greek literature. They have freedom and mobility. They're doing things on their own, even if they aren't things that society approves of. They're a struggling version of the people who make a difference in the world—the artists, the musicians, and the actors. I discover that I share a sensibility with them.

These older misfits give me a social circle. They tell me that the "cool" kids are just conventional people doing dumb things. I still have to contend with them because they're in school, but these new older friends convince me that I no longer need to worry about emulating my popular classmates. They offer relief because they absolve me of being an accessory in my own punishment.

We are inseparable the rest of the semester. They help me out of my self-loathing and I help them get their lives back on track. A lot of kids like this are defiant because they think nobody cares. I show them that somebody *does* care about them. My dad helps Bill find steady work, and my grandfather lets Dino sleep over when things get too hot at home. My parents open their arms to them, inviting them on weekend trips and including them at family gatherings. First to my amazement and then to my delight, my family find Bill and Dino as interesting and amusing as I do.

I have to hand it to my mom. She always tells me that when God closes one door, he opens another. As I sit curled up in the comfortable overstuffed chair in the family room talking to Annie on the phone, I realize that she's right.

"Annie, wait a minute, someone's calling on the other line. Hello?"

"Jodee, it's Ms. Linstrom."

"Hi!"

"I've got some wonderful news. I just received a letter from Eastern Illinois University. The judges were very impressed by your poetry. You won the scholarship for the summer writing workshop!"

"Oh, Ms. Linstrom, I'm so excited!"

"Come by my office on Monday and we'll fill out the paperwork."

"Thanks. See you then. Bye, Ms. Linstrom."

I click back to the other line.

"Annie, you'll never guess what happened!"

chapter eleven

An Unexpected Haven

I've been blessed. Despite getting knocked down so many times, God keeps putting people in my corner at just the right time who give me the courage and strength to come out for one more round. Often, the opponent isn't another fighter, but my own self-doubt. Though sometimes it feels like I'm alone in the ring, I know now that's an illusion. In the movie *Rocky* with Sylvester Stallone, no matter how badly Rocky gets hurt, he always has Mick (played by Burgess Meredith), believing in him. I have lots of Micks in my life—my parents and family, Annie and her crowd, my friends in Santorini, and caring adults such as Ms. Linstrom and Heleni.

I think about other outcasts, like Noreen, who don't have that kind of support. I wish I could help them. Their lives revolve around high school, but they need to realize that we'll graduate soon and the wounds we've sustained at the hands of our classmates will eventually heal and become scars.

When I asked Dr. Kalen about the human body's healing process, he told me that scar tissue is much stronger than regular skin. I believe the same is true of the human spirit. Some of the country's most successful people—musicians and moguls, authors and actors—were teen misfits, too. The heartache they endured at school defined their character and determination. Perhaps if they had it easy, they wouldn't have become who they are today.

When you're a victim of any kind of abuse, you can do one of two things. You can learn how to turn your pain into purpose and make a difference in the world, or you can allow it to extinguish the light inside you. If you permit the latter, you are sacrificing far more than your childhood to the cruel gods of popularity.

Today, I'm celebrating the fact that I've survived my junior year. Summer vacation is finally here, and my two-week speech and writing workshop begins tomorrow. Mom, dad, and I are driving down to Eastern Illinois University this afternoon.

"Jodee, let's get a move on," dad yells from the kitchen. "We've got a three-hour drive ahead of us."

"Coming," I call back to him, grabbing my knapsack and bounding downstairs.

My parents' love has sustained me through the years. Sometimes I lay in bed at night reflecting on the stress I've caused them. Though they never talk about it, I know my problems have put a strain on their marriage. I also believe that they blame themselves that I'm an outcast. Dad feels the most guilt. I think he worries that if he hadn't been away from home so much when I was growing up, maybe things would have been different. What he and mom don't recognize is that I'm my own person and always have been. They couldn't have changed who I am even if they had wanted to. Mom and dad accomplished something important, however. They taught me self-respect and compassion for others by setting a strong example of both. Not once in my life have I questioned whether or not they love me. There have been moments when I don't believe I am worthy of their love. But I never, ever worry that they'll stop loving me. I wish I could do more for them.

"What are you daydreaming about?" mom asks as we're loading up the car.

"What? Oh, nothing. I was just thinking about how much I love you and daddy."

"We love you, too, angel," dad says.

The drive to the university is pleasant. We talk about the future for the entire trip. I'll be starting senior year in the fall, and they're eager for me to choose a college. I've applied to several, so we'll see what happens. I have my SAT test scores: I did poorly in math and science, scoring in the lower 80th percentile for Samuels's district, but my English scores were among the top in the state.

"Are you nervous about this workshop?" mom asks as we merge onto route 294, traffic whizzing by us on all sides.

"No, I'm excited," I reply. "I think I'll have a lot in a common with the other kids there."

"Remember, honey, if you want to come back home, just pick up the phone and call us," dad says.

"I know, daddy. I will. But it's only two weeks. I'm sure everything will be fine."

The sun is starting to set by the time we arrive at Eastern. The campus is open and airy. Meticulously tended lawns and verdant gardens surround a series of beautiful modern buildings with large glass windows. Everything here feels shiny and new. "This place is great," I remark. "It's so cheerful and bright."

"I think this is going to be a wonderful experience for you," dad says, pulling into the lot marked "Dormitory Parking Only." "There's the dorm," mom says, pointing to the white brick structure on our left. "Let's get you settled in."

We walk in to a flurry of activity. Several long tables have been positioned in the main lobby of the dorm. A group of graduate students wearing badges that say "Dorm Monitor" are checking in the workshop participants. I go to the table marked "Names A–F" to fill out the paperwork. As I'm being handed a package with my room assignment, a six-foot-tall girl clad in tight jeans and a Peter Frampton T-shirt approaches me. "Hi, I'm Diana," she says. "Are you Jodee? I overheard your name when you were checking in. I think we're roommates."

"Yes, I'm Jodee. Hi!"

"Check your room assignment. Aren't you in 303?" Diana asks.

"Wait a sec, let me look," I answer, opening the envelope I'd just been handed. "Yep, 303! Mom, dad, come here. I want you to meet my roommate. This is Diana."

"It's good to meet you," mom says.

"It's nice meeting you, too," Diana responds.

"Where are you from?" dad asks.

"The southern part of the state, near Champagne. I won this scholarship for a poem I wrote and recited at our school speech tournament," she informs us. "This is the first time I've ever been away from home without my parents. They left about a half-hour ago."

"Come to think of it, this is the first time for me, too," I say.

"You girls are going to be fine," dad says, smiling. "Enjoy yourselves."

I hug my parents goodbye. As I watch them walk out to their car, it occurs to me that I'm growing up, and soon, my peers will be adults. It's finally starting to sink in that the past is almost behind me now. The next time I move into a dorm, it won't be for two weeks, but for four years of college. All I have to do is endure one more year of high school.

I adore it here at Eastern. The days are full and interesting. There are twenty of us in the program. We have composition and dramatic interpretation classes each morning, and rehearse our presentations during the afternoons. In the evenings, we hang out and talk and listen to music.

I've even met a guy who makes me swoon. His name is Tim. He's not drop-dead gorgeous in the traditional sense, but his personality is enticing. He's confident and strong and makes me feel beautiful every time he looks at me. The girls here are nuts about him. And yet, I'm the one he has a crush on. I hope he'll kiss me. As far as I'm concerned, I've never had a proper first kiss. In the sixth grade, when Peter and Steve planted those wet, clumsy smooches on me during that awful game of Spin the Bottle at Callie's party, it turned into disaster. Besides, there's nothing romantic about a dare. And in Santorini, Yorgos kissed me, but it was more brotherly than passionate.

Diana and I are becoming good friends. At first I try to hide my breast problem from her, going into the bathroom and shutting the door whenever I have to change my clothes. But tonight, while we're reviewing our notes from class, she starts telling me that she's always been an outcast, too. She shares how she's been picked on and taunted since seventh grade because of her height. "It got to the point that I refused to get out of bed. My parents ended up taking me to a shrink to get me to return to school," Diana confesses. "I've never felt like I fit in with other kids my age. If it wasn't for my writing, I don't know what I'd do."

"I understand all too well," I respond, taking my special bra out of the secret compartment in my suitcase and handing it to her. She examines it carefully. Then, she opens the top drawer of our dresser, folds it neatly, and places it inside.

"No more undressing in the john because you're embarrassed about your chest, okay? When I was in junior high, my posture was so horrible that my doctor was worried I would become hunchbacked. He even took x-rays of my spine to make sure I didn't have a bone disease. I slouched because I thought it would make me shrink. I still slump sometimes, but now I catch myself and pull back my shoulders. If I can learn not to be ashamed of looking like the Jolly Green Giant, you can learn to accept your body, too," she says.

I soon discover that Diana isn't the only one at this workshop who knows what it's like to be different. Almost everyone here is a teen misfit. One of our ongoing assignments is to keep a daily "memory journal." We're supposed to record important events from our pasts that continue to intrude on our present. The purpose of this exercise is to learn how to draw from personal experience to become a better storyteller.

The next morning a bunch of us are sitting outside in

the garden, reading to each other from our journals. I am both comforted and saddened as I listen to my companions describe how they, too, were abused and shunned. The two that touch me could almost be describing my own story.

Perry, who's got the most incredible blond hair and blue eyes I've ever seen, struggles to keep from breaking down as he reads a particularly painful passage:

Life was perfect until junior year. That's when it all came crashing down. I was on the football team and dating a cheerleader. All my friends were bragging about how often they were getting laid. They'd ask me if my girlfriend Sarah was "good in the sack" and I'd just stare at them and not say anything. I didn't dare tell them we still hadn't "done it" yet. It wasn't like in the movies, where the girl didn't want to go all the way but the guy was pressuring her. With Sarah and I, it was the opposite. All her friends were losing their virginity at warp speed and she didn't want to be left out. We agreed to "go all the way" Saturday night at her house when her parents would be visiting her sister at college. When I got to Sarah's, she answered the door in tight jeans and her sexiest sweater. She kissed me, gliding her tongue along the edges of my mouth. She led me to the couch and we began undressing each other. We were necking hot and heavy. She told me not to worry, that she was wearing a diaphragm. I asked if she was sure about this. She hesitated, then told me it didn't matter whether or not she felt ready, because if she remained a virgin much longer all her friends would start to make fun of her. That's when I stopped. My parents had always taught me that sex is a big step and should be something two people share who love each other and who are truly ready. I wasn't sure Sarah and I qualified on either front.

I said, "Sarah, we can't have sex because you're worried that your friends won't think you're cool anymore unless we do. I don't want to do this, not now, anyway." Sarah was furious. "How can you do this to me?" she screamed. "My reputation is fucked!" I couldn't help but think how much the world had changed since the era of Happy Days. *"Better your reputation than you by someone you're not in love with," I responded, walking out. By the next day, everyone at school had heard Sarah's version of what happened. A varsity football player's extremely hot-looking girlfriend was lying naked on the couch begging to be laid, and the loser couldn't even get it up. He must be a fag. I would walk down the halls and people would start shouting "wimp" and "dickless wonder." It was awful. I wanted to crawl into a hole and die. Things got so bad for me after that, I quit the football team. I don't know what'll happen senior year. I try not to think about it.* ■

Next, Carol, a brunette who looks like an exotic Romanian gypsy, begins to read.

I don't know why we have to keep a memory journal about things we'd probably be much better off forgetting. . . .

Several people nod their heads in agreement.

I don't know what to write. I've always hated school. While my classmates fantasize about rock stars and dating, I'm reading about past lives and haunted houses. I've always loved the idea of ghosts and the possibility that we can communicate with them. When I was little, spirits visited me in my dreams and told me things before they happened. It used to freak out my parents. When that Pan Am flight crashed several years ago, I told my mom the day before that a big jet was going to explode in the sky. My grandmother was psychic. She was born and raised in the old country. People would come to her from all over to ask about their futures. She said I have the gift of second sight, too. I've tried to be a normal high school student, but it never works. I think teenagers are unusually perceptive. They know when you're trying to be someone you're not. I went to Homecoming this year with a friend of my brother's. He didn't want to take me but my brother forced him into it. I wish he hadn't. When we got to the dance, a bunch of girls from my homeroom started yelling at my date, "Hey, you're cute. Why are you with the school witch? Did she cast a spell on you?" I was mortified. I felt like Carrie from the Stephen King novel. You know how I got this scholarship? I wrote a poem about how dying wouldn't be any big change because I was already half dead inside. It was a suicide note. After my parents rushed me to the hospital to get my stomach pumped, they showed the poem they found next to my bed to my teacher. She submitted it to the scholarship committee and that's why I'm here. At first I didn't want to come. But now I love being

*here. Being different back home can hurt you. Here,
people like you for it. I wish we never had to go home
again.* ■

Carol's reading moves us. Tim, who's sitting next to me,
reaches over and squeezes her hand. Then, he begins to read.

*I feel so weird being at this workshop. Almost everyone
I've met here are people who my friends and I would
make fun of like crazy if they went to our school.* ■

Suddenly, Tim closes his journal and stops reading.

"What is it, why have you stopped?" I ask.

"Because I'm ashamed of what I wrote and I don't want
to read it to you," he responds.

"I don't understand. Why?" Diana asks.

"Yeah Tim, be honest with us. We won't judge you.
Right, everyone?" Carol says.

"I don't want to read you what I've written because it
doesn't reflect how I feel anymore. I've always been really
popular at school. I didn't want to attend this workshop. I
got roped into it by my English teacher, who basically told
me that if I didn't do it, I wouldn't make honors next year.
When I first got here, I thought it was unfair that someone
as cool as me would have to hang out with the nerds and
outcasts. That's how my friends and I are. If you're not in
our clique, you're nothing. After I started getting to know
each of you, I realized what jerks we've been. At school, it's
always so much pressure to act cool all the time. Here, I can
just be me, and no one puts me down for it. Anyhow, that's

why I don't want to read you what I've written. It's no longer true. I'm really glad I'm here."

"Thanks, Tim," Diana says.

"Look at the time," Carol remarks. "We better get moving or we'll be late."

"Hey, Jodee, wait up," Tim says, grabbing my hand. "Can I walk you to class?"

I nearly faint with glee. "Sure," I reply.

Hours later, after we've all eaten dinner, Tim asks if I'd like to take a stroll with him through the campus gardens. As we walk arm in arm through the fragrant summer foliage, we talk about our lives. I share with him some of what I've gone through these past few years. At one point, I am near tears as I recount the incident in the locker room. He hugs me and tells me that I'm the most appealing girl he's ever met. Then, he leans toward me and kisses me, gently at first, then harder, more passionately. His tongue probes the inside of my mouth. My whole body is tingling. This moment couldn't be more perfect. As Tim and I make our way back toward the dorm, I know that whatever lies ahead senior year, I am ready for it now. Here at Eastern, a handful of kindred spirits found a brief and unexpected haven from their hell. I will never forget these two weeks.

chapter twelve

The Reconstructionist

Since returning from the writer's workshop, I have a renewed sense of self. I'm not naïve. I know that there are challenges ahead of me, but at least now I can face them without wishing I were dead. I never want to feel that way about myself again.

While I was at Eastern, the doctors from the Mayo Clinic called my parents and said they could schedule my surgery for July. Mom and dad surprised me with the news on the drive home from Eastern. Now, here we are in the car again, this time making our way to Minnesota where Mayo Clinic is located. I'm scared—I've never been in the hospital overnight before, let alone to be operated on. I know I have to do this because I can't go through life with my breasts the way they are. But the idea of having them sliced open, rebuilt, and then sewn back onto my chest is unnerving.

"Honey, it'll be over before you know it," mom says reassuringly. "You'll be a new person afterward."

"I know you're probably right, but I'm still scared," I admit.

"It's natural to be afraid," dad says. "We're not going to force you into anything. This is your decision."

"Daddy, there's no alternative. I'm in pain. I'm deformed."

"It'll be all right," mom soothes.

"We're in Rochester," dad announces, pulling into the parking lot of the Marriott Hotel. "We still have a few hours before our appointment with Dr. Arnold. Let's check in and walk around a bit to get our bearings."

I'm not in the mood to go exploring, but maybe it's better to keep busy right now. Mom says that Mayo Clinic has taken a special interest in my case because it's so unusual. I guess that's good, but I can't help longing for the day when I'm normal.

The Mayo Clinic is a city unto itself. Considered one of the premier medical facilities in the world, it looks like something out of a futuristic movie. It encompasses almost the entire town of Rochester, Minnesota. The clinic's buildings are connected through miles of underground tunnels that make you feel as if you're at an upscale mall on a warm, sunny afternoon. There are dozens of shops and restaurants, all brightly lit with elegant art on the walls, and friendly, smiling employees eager to make you as comfortable as possible.

As we stroll past a boutique, dad sees me gazing longingly at a lingerie display in the window. "Honey, in just a few weeks you'll be able to wear things like that," he says, pointing to the lacy undergarments. "No more clumsy straps and buckles."

I have to stop thinking about the operation and concentrate on what I'll look like afterward. Imagine not being afraid to let a boy touch me under my shirt because I'm worried he'll be repulsed. I won't have to undress in the dark or hide in bathroom stalls anymore. How I ache to see myself naked in a mirror and be able to say I'm not ugly anymore.

"It's almost two. Dr. Arnold will be waiting," mom says, glancing at her watch.

While we're walking to his office, I focus on finding the courage to go through with this. The moment we enter his waiting room, Leah, Dr. Arnold's assistant, a lovely nurse born and raised in the Philippines, greets us.

"Hello. You must be Jodee," she says warmly. "Dr. Arnold is anxious to meet you."

"Thank you. But I'm really nervous."

"Don't be. There's nothing to worry about. You're in very good hands here. Dr. Arnold is a brilliant surgeon. You couldn't have found a more dedicated doctor," Leah remarks.

"That makes me feel better."

"That's good. Mr. and Mrs. Blanco, please, why don't you and Jodee come with me."

Leah leads us down a long hall to an office with a sign on the door that reads "Dr. Arnold, Chief of Plastic and Reconstructive Surgery."

"I didn't know he was chief of surgery," I remark.

"Only the best for our daughter," dad replies, smiling.

When Dr. Arnold walks in, I'm pleased by what I see. Big and burly with broad shoulders and twinkling blue eyes, he immediately makes me feel at ease.

"So, you're Jodee," he says, cupping my chin with the palm of his hand. "We're going to make you as beautiful on the outside as you are on the inside."

"It's good to meet you," I reply, touched by his concern.

"And you must be Jodee's parents," he says. "I know you have questions. Let me take a look at Jodee in the examining room, and then we can sit down and I'll explain the procedure in detail."

"That would be fine, doctor," mom replies.

"Come on, Jodee, this will only take a few minutes," Dr. Arnold says. "It'll be painless, I promise."

I'm led to a small, brightly lit examining room. Medical diagrams hang on all the walls. I remove my shirt and bra and place them at my side. Taking his thumb and forefinger, he begins squeezing the flesh around both my breasts, and then the nipples. Next, he removes a ballpoint pen from his pocket.

"This might tickle," he says.

"What are you going to do?" I ask.

"I'm going to mark the areas where I'll be making the incisions so that I can show you and your parents exactly what I'll be doing," he answers.

"You're right, it does tickle," I tell him.

"Please put this gown on and I'll be right back with your mom and dad," Dr. Arnold says.

For the next hour, Dr. Arnold patiently answers all our questions. He says that I have what's referred to as "tubular, asymmetric breasts." A small percentage of young women develop abnormally, but the severity of my condition is rare. There is no known cause. Research indicates that it's a congenital birth defect that remains undetectable until puberty. He reiterates that I will not grow out of it, and that reconstructive surgery is the only solution. He explains that the first step will be a photo session, during which a medical photographer will shoot my "before" pictures. Stills will also be shot of the actual procedure, and then "after" pictures will be taken. Dr. Arnold explains that it's important to keep a detailed visual record of each patient.

When dad asks Dr. Arnold how long he anticipates I'll be in surgery, the answer chills me to the bone: six to eight hours. I can feel my courage slipping away. What a choice. Go through life looking like a circus freak or be drugged into darkness and cut open. Dr. Arnold sees the look on my face and gives me a gentle, reassuring hug.

"Jodee, your imagination is making this scarier than it really is," he says. "You'll be in and out of the hospital in three days, and back home watching television before you know it."

I ask him to walk my parents and me through the procedure itself. He gently opens the top of the hospital gown I'm wearing, and points to the pen marks on my breasts. He explains that he's going to do a reduction on the right breast, and put an implant in the left breast so that they become uniform in size. The nipples will also have to be reconstructed. Retracing his pen marks, he shows us the five incisions he'll make on the right breast and the three he'll do on the left breast. I question him about scarring. He tells me yes, I will have significant scars. There's no way to avoid it, he explains. Then he drops the final bomb. He says that one surgery will not completely correct my problem. Though my appearance will improve radically, I will likely require one more operation when I'm in my late twenties or early thirties because my body will mature and change.

"If I'm going to need surgery again in ten years, why don't I just wait?" I cry.

"You could wait, but do you really want to continue being uncomfortable with how you look when it's unnecessary?"

Dr. Arnold replies.

"Honey, the doctor is right. You can't go on like this for another decade," dad says.

"Okay, I'll do it," I announce.

"Leah will make all the arrangements," Dr. Arnold says. "I'd like to schedule surgery for the day after tomorrow."

Less than thirty-six hours later, I'm in anesthesiology, reclining on what looks like a chair in a dentist's office. There are technicians in lab coats standing all around me. One of them places a mask over my face and instructs me to breathe deeply. As I inhale the sweet-tasting air, I grow woozy and my vision starts to blur. Somebody ties a rubber tourniquet around my right arm. Suddenly, I feel a pinprick. I try to speak, but can't because of the mask. I panic. A nurse grabs my hand and squeezes it, telling me everything's going to be all right—soon I will wake up and this will all seem like a dream. Then, I slip into unconsciousness . . .

The next thing I know, I'm in a large room. The light is blinding. There are rows of patients lying on gurneys, just like me. I hear monitors beeping and smell antiseptic. Nurses in crisp white uniforms are buzzing all around me. I'm being fed some sort of clear liquid through an intravenous needle in my wrist. My chest is on fire. Gingerly, I place my left hand on my breasts. They feel stiff and spongy and I realize they are bandaged. Gathering my strength, I raise my head and look down at my chest, peeking under the surgical gown. Bright red splotches of blood have soaked through the gauze. I scream, but all that comes out is a whimper. "Where's my mom?" I cry. "I want my mom." One of the nurses rushes over to me.

"You'll see your mom in just a few minutes," she says, her voice calm, yet warm. "You did wonderfully well in surgery. Dr. Arnold wants to look at you, and then I'll take you to your room."

"It's all over?" I ask, groggily.

"Yes, dear," she says, patting my hand.

As the week passes, it's not so much the pain that's bothering me, but the itching. All I can think about is scratching the sutures. It's driving me out of my skin. On Friday morning, when Dr. Arnold comes by to remove the bandages, I fantasize about taking my hairbrush and running it across my incisions.

My parents are standing next to my hospital bed. Dr. Arnold and Leah begin peeling the bandages off, then the gauze. The process pulls slightly on my stitches, bringing welcome relief from the itching.

"Close your eyes, Jodee, and don't open them until I tell you," Dr. Arnold says.

"Oh, my God, Tony," mom gasps.

"What?" I ask, gulping.

"Okay," Dr. Arnold says, placing a mirror in my hands. "Open your eyes."

There are no words to describe how I feel as I look at my reflection. Part of me is completely grossed out by the freshness of the wounds. Rows of black stitches caked with bits of dried blood form a circle around each nipple and line the base of both breasts. There's significant bruising down the side of my chest, almost to the underarm. Though the trauma of seeing myself like this is upsetting, I am elated at the miracle before me. My breasts are finally the same size!

They're plump and round and beautiful.

"I'm not ugly anymore! You've changed my life, Dr. Arnold. Daddy, thank you so much for this." By now, my parents and I are all in tears. Even Dr. Arnold's eyes are moist.

Within a few hours, mom, dad and I are on the road again. When we return home, Bill, Dino, Annie, and her brother David are waiting at the house for us. They've hung a banner that reads: "Welcome Back, Beautiful."

I spend the rest of the summer recuperating. Evie and my other aunts take turns helping my mom and grand-mother take care of me. One evening after my stitches have been removed, dad asks if I'd like to go to the mall.

"Sure," I reply. "What are we shopping for?"

"It's a surprise," he says.

We go directly to Marshall Field's. Taking my hand, he leads me up the escalators, past the women's clothing section to the lingerie department. "Honey, you don't have to wear those clunky bras anymore," dad says. "Miss, my daughter needs some help. I'll be sitting right over there if anyone wants me," he says to the sales lady. An older woman with a kind disposition spends the next two hours fitting me with pretty bras and underwear.

As dad and I are driving back home, I hug my bag of purchases. "Oh, daddy, thank you so much! I feel like this is the first time I've ever really noticed the daylight before."

"You're welcome, angel," he replies, his voice brusque with emotion.

I can't wait to start senior year in my new body!

chapter thirteen

The Turning Point

The summer flew by. It's the first day of my last year of high school. I feel like I've been a prisoner and my sentence is nearly up. I wonder if anyone will notice the change in my body. Most of my classmates will probably think I've been working out. Gym isn't going to be an issue this year. Dr. Arnold and the legal department at the Mayo Clinic wrote a strong letter to the school board demanding that Ms. Nichols release me from physical ed or be held liable should I suffer any injuries. No more sitting on the bleachers, either. I've been issued a library pass instead.

Whatever happens this year, I know I can handle it. There's a rainbow over the horizon: graduation. If things get bad between now and then, I'll focus on the future. My parents are taking me to New York over Christmas break to visit some universities on the East Coast, and I have Santorini to look forward to next summer. Annie and her friends are here for me, too. I mustn't crack like I did last year. I have to keep reminding myself that none of this will matter when I'm an adult. It will all be just shadows.

"Honey, you better hurry up. It's nearly eight A.M.," mom yells from the kitchen.

"I'll be right there," I respond. Coming down the stairs, I smell bacon sizzling in the frying pan and fresh-brewed coffee.

"What about breakfast?"

"Sounds great," I reply.

"Are you nervous about today?" she asks.

"A little, I guess. But at least I'll be driving myself to school."

Dad never breaks a promise. When Heleni told him how well I was progressing with my Greek lessons, dad gave me one of his company cars to use, a blue Chevy Citation. I enjoy the independence of having a car. It also gives me a sense of safety because I know that if anyone tries to hurt me at school, I have a means of immediate escape.

"And remember, one year from now, you'll be in a brand-new place. Look what a wonderful experience you had at Eastern. College will be even better," mom says, handing me an egg and bacon sandwich.

"I'll be okay," I reassure her. "For the first time in years, I'm not ashamed of how I look. That makes a big difference."

As I'm driving to school, I think about the future. Though I realize mom's right, that twelve months from now my entire world will change, I still can't help feeling trepidation about senior year. Just because I have new breasts doesn't mean my classmates will have a new attitude toward me. I pull into Samuels's parking lot. I turn off the motor and sit in the car for several minutes before finally opening the door and getting out. When I enter the main building, I notice the familiar blue-and-gold football banner hanging on the back wall. That's odd. The words "Samuels Hell" are stitched across the emblem. I haven't even been back for ten minutes, but already my mind is playing tricks on me.

When I look again, I realize it says "Samuels Hawks."

"Hey, Jodee, did you lose weight?" a friendly voice inquires. I turn around and see Nadia clad in her cheerleading outfit, bouncing toward me like some surreal rubber ball.

"Obviously, *you* didn't get any thinner," I reply, staring directly at her thighs, trying to make her squirm.

"Hey, screw you Blanco, I was just trying to be nice," she retorts angrily.

"Nice? What happened, did you suddenly grow a kindness gene over the summer?"

"What are you talking about?" she asks.

"You don't remember what you and Mark and a bunch of other jerks did to me that day after gym last semester?" I ask her.

"What, you mean when we teased you about being a virgin?" Nadia recalls. "Wait a minute, *that's* what's different about you. You had a boob job!"

"I did not!" I answer. "I've been lifting weights, that's all."

"You're lying. You had some kind of work done," she insists. "It's okay if you did. Lots of people fix stuff about their bodies they don't like. Besides, weren't your tits all weird and uneven?"

"I don't get it, Nadia. Why are you talking to me now and trying to be nice after what happened before? Why the sudden change?"

"Jodee, you're too serious. Yeah, we teased you. So what? It's not like you're the first person to be made fun of at this school. Somebody like you never fights back. Why do you take it, anyway? You're not a stupid fat ass like Noreen.

You could have stood up for yourself. Why didn't you fight back and tell us to go screw ourselves or something?"

"Nadia, what you did was not teasing. You guys were cruel."

"So what? Everybody at school knows that if they pick on you, you'll take it. It's your own fault," Nadia comments.

"You don't know what it's like to be taunted all the time," I remark. "You've always been popular. It's easy for you to tell me to fight back when you've never been in a situation like that."

"No, but if I was, I wouldn't be a wimp ass like you and let people piss all over me, that's for sure," she says, walking off.

The truth hurts. I can't stand Nadia, and she doesn't like me either. But it doesn't change the fact that she's right. The next time people at this school decide to mess with me, they're going to be in for one hell of a lesson.

The first few weeks of senior year pass swiftly. Surprisingly, no one is giving me a hard time. I should be happy and relieved, but instead, it makes me suspicious. There's an old cliché: "If it seems too good to be true, it probably is." That's exactly how I feel. It's like the moment in a horror movie before the slasher strikes. At least when I was getting teased and taunted, I knew what to expect.

Am I going to be this way for the rest of my life, always waiting for something bad to happen? Will I never truly be able to trust anyone? I worry that when I'm older, I'll be so afraid that people won't like me that I'll have trouble believing it when they actually do. What if the popular kids at college accept me? Will I blow it because I'm unable to believe that the cool crowd could actually like me? Intellectually, I recognize that I'm being ridiculous, but in my gut, it all makes perfect sense. Here I am, nervous and afraid because I'm *not* being abused. I've finally flipped.

"Jodee, what are you daydreaming about?" Annie asks, approaching me by the lockers.

"You're going to think this is nuts," I tell her.

"Try me," she responds.

"I'm uncomfortable because no one's been mean to me lately."

"I don't get it. I thought that's what you wanted," Annie says.

"It is," I respond.

"Then what's the problem?" she asks.

"I don't know. Something just doesn't feel right," I answer.

"You're paranoid."

"You're right. Maybe Jacklyn and A.J. and those guys finally got bored of giving me a hard time," I reply. "Let's just drop the subject."

"Fine by me," Annie says. "We better get moving. By the way, can you come over to my house tonight, say around five o'clock? There's somebody I want to fix you up with."

"Who? You can't just tell me something like that and then walk away. I'll be dying of curiosity all day!"

"His name is Andre," she responds, smiling. "That's all I'm going to say until you meet him!"

I've never been on a blind date before. In fact, other than Tim and Yorgos, I've never really had any kind of boyfriend. I find that it's impossible to concentrate the rest of the afternoon. All I can think about is tonight.

When I arrive at Annie's that evening, she flings open the front door before I even get out of my car. "Come on, he'll be here any minute," she says. "I want to see how you look."

"Do I pass inspection?"

"Definitely. Now, do you want me to tell you about this guy?"

"Yes, I've been waiting all day!" I reply.

"First of all, he's a total babe. You're going to flip when you see what he looks like," she says.

"How old is he?" I ask.

"He's turning twenty-two in a couple of months," Annie answers.

"I didn't realize he was that much older than me."

"Only four years. Besides, you're mature for your age. That's probably why you've never clicked with any of the guys at school," Annie observes.

"How do you know Andre?" I ask.

"He and my brother work together," she says.

"Oh, he's a construction worker?"

"Actually, he's the foreman on David's site. You two are going to hit it off. I can feel it."

Just then, the doorbell rings. "He's here!" Annie exclaims.

She wasn't exaggerating about his appearance. Tall and muscular, with black hair and blue bedroom eyes, he's wearing a tight T-shirt and Levi's. He reminds me of that new movie star, Mel Gibson. "Hi. Annie's told me such great things about you," I say. Though I'm composed on the out-side, my stomach is doing flip-flops.

"Hello," he responds, flashing me a warm smile.

"Why don't we all go downstairs?" Annie suggests. "You guys go ahead. I'll get us something to drink, then be right down."

Andre and I curl up in the big overstuffed couch in the family room. By the time Annie rejoins us, we're immersed in conversation. Tonight is everything I had imagined. Nothing is awkward between Andre and me. I like this guy— I hope he asks me out for a date.

It turns out that he doesn't just ask me out, he and I end up dating for several months. At first, my parents are concerned about the age difference, but Andre's endearing personality soon puts them at ease. He's never late when he picks me up, and he always gets me back home early. He and my dad often have long chats about everything from football to music. I love spending time with Andre. I get goosebumps whenever the phone rings, thinking it might be him.

My relationship with Andre deepens. We're together at least two nights a week and most of the weekend. We neck and I let him touch me under my clothes. I've even shown him my scars. He says that I should never be ashamed of them, and he teases me that I've got "perfect melons." One night, we're kissing on the floor and things start to heat up.

"Andre, don't."

"Come on, we've been dating for months," he replies, gently nibbling my earlobe.

"I'm not ready to go all the way yet. You know I'm a virgin," I respond.

"I'm sorry. I didn't mean to push you. But I don't know how much I can take of this," he complains. "Maybe I should date someone my own age. I think you're too young for me," he observes.

"Andre, please don't say that."

"Jodee, you know I care for you. It's not because I don't respect you, it's because I do that I think it might be better if we break up," he says.

"Would you still take me to the Homecoming dance? It would mean so much to me." By now, I'm crying hard. He takes me into his arms. Rocking me gently back and forth, he tells me that he wouldn't miss Homecoming for the world.

The eve of Homecoming, I'm as jittery as a cat. It's tough to be around Andre under such romantic circumstances, yet know that after tonight, we'll be out of each other's lives for good. On top of that, I don't trust my classmates. They've been a little *too* civil to me lately. I shouldn't have watched the movie *Carrie* over the weekend. It's making my imagination run wild. I'm worried they'll embarrass me at the dance in front of Andre. Tonight will be taxing enough without that added pressure.

When Andre arrives to pick me up, I bite my tongue to prevent myself from crying. He looks gorgeous in his tuxedo. He hands me an exquisite corsage and my parents shoot several rolls of film. Everything about this night is perfect, except instead of it being a promise of things to come, it's a farewell.

The gym is decorated in vibrant shades of blue and gold. There are streamers everywhere, and glitter sprinkled across the floor. The D.J. is playing "Time for Me to Fly," by REO Speedwagon. Struck by the irony of the D.J.'s choice of song, Andre and I just look at each other. "Let's dance," he suggests. As we make our way to the floor, Jacklyn approaches us with several members of her entourage in tow. She's wearing a short red cocktail dress and high heels.

"Who's this?" she asks, staring at Andre. "Isn't he a little too old to be dating a virgin?"

"Screw you," I reply. "Come on Andre, let's go."

"What did you say?" Jacklyn asks.

"You heard me. I said screw you."

"Hey, babe, take it easy," Andre says, draping his arm protectively around my shoulder and turning to Jacklyn. "May I have your card?"

"What?" she responds, perplexed.

"I'm throwing a bachelor party for my buddy next week and I may be interested in using your services," he explains, giving my arm a subtle squeeze.

"What are you talking about?" Jacklyn asks, still confused.

"Hiring you," Andre says.

"You think I'm a *hooker*?" she cries, nearly breaking a nail trying to pull down her dress. Her eyes dart nervously around the room as if seeking an escape. Her friends snicker.

"Well, yes. Aren't you?"

"No!" she declares, horrified.

I've never seen Jacklyn humiliated or embarrassed before. I'm enjoying every second of it. "Sorry ma'am, my mistake," Andre says, taking my hand and leading me to the dance floor.

"That was amazing!" I tell Andre, barely able to control my glee. "That was *so* great."

"It was, wasn't it?" Andre says, smiling. "Now, let's have that dance."

Winter arrives in full force, casting a snowy blanket across the entire Midwest. Though I try to remain cheerful and upbeat, I miss Andre terribly. Mom and dad are taking me to New York City this weekend. I have interviews at two universities in Pennsylvania, so dad thought it would be fun to visit Manhattan for a couple of days, then rent a car and drive to Pennsylvania. He's eager for me to experience the city where he was born and raised. He says we'll be staying in an area called Greenwich Village, which he says I'm going to love. One of his clients has a corporate apartment off a big park there called Washington Square that he's offered to let us use.

The flight to La Guardia is pleasant. Within an hour of landing, we're in our rental car, driving through the teeming Manhattan streets. Dad is playing tour guide, pointing out various landmarks. "That's Rockefeller Center," he says, gesturing toward an enormous conglomeration of high-rise buildings, retail stores, and colorful gardens. "Over there is Radio City Music Hall. That's where the Rockettes perform," he continues, so happy to be sharing this with mom and me.

"Where are we now?" I ask.

"We're on Fifth Avenue going down toward Washington

Square," dad informs me. As we wind around the park, I am fascinated by the lively environment. "Is this the Village?" I ask, eager to get out of the car and walk around.

"Yes, honey," dad says, pulling into a garage underneath a red brick apartment building. "This is where we'll be staying. Let's drop off our bags, and I'll take you girls on a New York adventure."

For the next two days, dad introduces mom and me to New York. I fall in love with Manhattan, especially the Village. Sunday afternoon, as we're sitting on a bench in Washington Square Park eating bagels with cream cheese, I suddenly get an inspiration. "You said that all these buildings around the park are part of New York University, right?"

"Yes, honey. This is the heart of NYU's campus," he explains.

"Look at the people in this park, dad. I would fit in here, I just know it. Please, I want to go to school here."

"Honey, are you sure? You wouldn't be living on a traditional campus. And New York is a tough city," he says.

"It can't be any tougher than what I've already gone through," I reply. "Dad, I know I'm meant to go to school here. I've never been so sure about anything in my whole life."

"Jodee, I'm not sure you'll get accepted," mom cautions.

"I'll get in, mom. I just have to."

We still visit the colleges in Pennsylvania, but as we tour the campuses, my mind is racing with thoughts of NYU and what it will be like to live in New York. When we return to Chicago, I send in my application. Ten days later, I get a letter from the dean's office explaining that NYU has recently started a new liberal arts program specifically designed for students interested in creative writing and history. They submitted my application to their admissions board, and I've been accepted. The letter goes on to say that it's an exclusive program, with only twelve to fifteen students per classroom. "See! I told you, I'm meant to go to NYU," I tell my parents as I jump up and down.

Getting accepted at NYU is the best Christmas gift anyone could have given me, so the holidays are bright and joyous this year. I even spend some time with Paul, who is home visiting from college. He tells me how proud he is of me. "Soon you'll be a college girl," he declares. "Your whole life will change."

As second semester rolls along, I find that high school is becoming less important to me. I'm still getting picked on, but it doesn't bother me like it used to. Everything about Samuels seems like yesterday to me. My focus is on tomorrow. I just got word from NYU that I've been assigned to live in the Rubin Dorm on Fifth Avenue. I can't believe it. I'm going to be studying in New York City, living on the swankest street in town.

I don't think the major events in a person's life are ever the result of chance. Things happen for a reason. I know that being rejected and hurt had a purpose in my life. Now I'm excited about learning what that purpose is.

I close my eyes and picture all the other outcasts I've known throughout my school years. I wonder what will become of us all. I'm one of the lucky ones because I'm full of hope for the future. It's no accident that all of this is on my mind right now. Earlier this week, something happened that made me see things more clearly than I ever have.

While I was sitting in study hall, my teacher announced that there would be a new student joining us for the remainder of the semester. She said his name was Dave, and he was a junior. Since our study hall had both juniors and seniors, I didn't think anything of it until he walked in the door. I couldn't believe my eyes. It was the same Dave I had gone to Morgan Hills Academy with, the same Dave who was the class nerd, the one Callie refused to let me invite to her party. As I stared at Dave, I wondered if he would recognize me. He certainly looked different. In sixth grade, he had been the epitome of a geek, with his thick glasses and clumsy, unsure ways. Now, the young man standing before me was what the older generation would call a "punk." Clad in ripped blue jeans, a Hell's Angels T-shirt, and an old beat-up leather biker jacket with a skull and crossbones emblem emblazoned on the back, Dave was an intimidating figure indeed. His hair was long and swept off his face with a red bandana, and he was wearing one earring in his left ear. Oddly enough, though everything about him was now radically changed, he still wore the thick glasses, and a residual nervousness lingered beneath his cold, angry veneer. Dave was the same scared little geek. The costume—and in my mind, that's what it was— was his armor against being hurt.

"Dave, it's Jodee, from Morgan Park."

Dave stared me down, then replied coolly, "Hi, Jodee."

"You look so different, I barely recognize you," I said, slightly uncomfortable.

"A lot has happened since sixth grade," he answers, his voice icy and calculating.

"What do you mean?"

"Let's just say that after Morgan Park, I got smart. I made sure no one ever teased me again."

"Why are you a junior? Shouldn't you be graduating now?" I ask.

"I got locked up for eight months in a juvenile detention center, so they held me back a year at school."

"That's awful."

"Nah, I don't care. I got my revenge. That's all that matters," he remarks.

I decided I didn't want to know any more.

After our exchange that day, though I did try to make conversation with him, it's no use. He's not rude, just short. I remind him of how he used to feel about himself, but he's spent the past six years of his life concocting a whole new persona to help him forget. I can't blame him for wanting to avoid me. It's not me he's running away from, it's what I represent to him.

Despite his appearance and his tough demeanor, this is a guy who could be a great man if he could learn to be vulnerable again. And then it strikes me. That's what being an outcast can cost you: your vulnerability. People tend to consider being vulnerable a bad thing. It's not. Vulnerability reminds us that we're human. It keeps us open to giving and receiving love. Without at least a little, we can become what Dave is trying so hard to be—someone living in a prison of our own making, where the walls are so thick that no one can get in or out.

The prom is only three weeks away. My parents think I should go, but I don't have a date. I thought about asking Paul, but he'll be in the middle of finals. I'm just about to give up on the idea when Annie's brother David calls.

"Hey, Jodee, are you going to prom with anyone?" David asks.

"No, why?"

"Well, you might think this is crazy, but I was wondering if you'd like to go with me," he inquires.

"That's so sweet of you to offer, but I didn't think prom was your kind of thing," I respond.

"What, you mean because I'm gay?" he answers.

"Well, yes," I reply.

"Don't be silly. Besides, you're my sister's best friend," he says.

"Did Annie put you up to this?" I ask.

"No, she didn't. She doesn't even know I was going to ask you," he says.

"David?"

"Yeah?"

"*Thanks.*"

When my parents find out I'm going to the prom with David, they're elated. "We better start moving," mom proclaims. She and grandmother spend days getting me ready. By the time prom night arrives, you'd think there was a film premiere being hosted in our living room, and we were all VIPs. Dad's manning the video camera, standing by the front door, ready to shoot footage of David from the moment he steps inside. Grandfather's ready with the Polaroid. Weddings require less of a fuss.

"Oh, he's here," mom says, jumping up to get the door.

David looks like a younger version of Nick Nolte. He hands me a beautiful corsage. For a moment, my mind drifts to Andre and the corsage he gave me for Homecoming. Pushing the memories away, I focus on David. He, Annie, Bill, and Dino have been good friends. I never want them to think that I take their friendship for granted.

Instead of the school gym, the prom is being held in a large banquet facility. When David and I arrive, we're immediately greeted by someone from the committee who hands us a place card with our table number on it. There's a live band playing classic rock-and-roll. There are three other couples, whom I know vaguely, at our table. One of the girls is in my English class. She asks if David and I have been going together for a long time. He explains that we're just good friends.

"You guys make such a cute couple, though," she remarks. "Best friends make the best lovers!"

I can sense that David is beginning to get uncomfortable. "Hey, I love this song, why don't we dance?" I suggest, pulling him onto the dance floor.

"What was *that* all about?" he comments.

"I think she was just being sociable," I reply, trying to defuse the tension.

David and I are still on the dance floor when the band shifts the mood, playing a set of ballads. As I watch the other couples nuzzling each other, I begin to feel . . . not depressed, exactly, but hollow. This is supposed to be one of the most romantic events in a teenager's life. Images of Andre flash before my eyes.

"You're thinking about Andre, aren't you?" David observes.

"Yes," I reply. "It's not so much about him. It's just, I wonder how I'll remember this night when I look back on it twenty years from now. That's all."

"I know what you mean," he says.

"Let's just dance and enjoy being together. That's the most important thing."

"You're right," David agrees.

The rest of the evening, we dance and talk. I realize that the friendship David and I share is as strong and real as the affection holding together most of the relationships in this room.

After the prom, there are only three weeks left before graduation, and they zip by. The last day of school, I feel utter relief. Everyone in the senior class is busy signing each other's yearbooks. I can't bear the thought of not having any signatures. What kind of a keepsake will it be? I figure if I only ask a few people to sign mine and avoid the popular crowd, I'll be okay. I still have a crush on Tyler. He hasn't picked on me this year, so I decide to take a leap of faith. It takes me an hour to muster up the courage, but I finally ask him if he'll write something nice. He smiles and says he'd be honored. I'm thrilled! What a wonderful way to end my senior year.

When he hands back my yearbook, there, in black

indelible marker, scribbled in capital letters are the words:

YOU'LL HAVE TO FUCK YOURSELF,
WE HATE YOU, BITCH.

It's as if someone has kicked me in the chest. The self-esteem I have worked so hard to protect all year turns to dust. Clutching the yearbook with one hand, and covering my face with the other, I run out of Samuels, jump in my car and drive away. That's the last time I ever see the inside of my high school again.

chapter fourteen

The Reunion

I'm still sitting in a rented Pontiac in the parking lot of the Hilton Hotel in Chicago Heights. For an hour, I've been trying to muster the courage to walk through those banquet doors. I even made a mental list of every celebrity I've ever worked with, as well as the titles of all the books and movies I've done publicity for, thinking that if I consciously remind myself how much a part of the *real* cool crowd I am in New York and Los Angeles, it will make facing the "cool" crowd from high school all those years ago less scary. I keep telling myself that if I could talk boxing over coffee with Muhammad Ali, share a crème brûlée with Mickey Rooney, and sip tea with the Ukrainian ambassador, I should certainly be able to handle a quick trip down memory lane with a few former classmates. Yet, I'm rooted to the pavement.

And you'd think I'd be okay with all this. Four years ago, I not only survived another reunion, but it had been one of the most astonishing experiences of my life. It was my twentieth grammar school reunion. Although I had left Holy Ascension in tears back in the sixth grade, never to return, my mother received an invitation for me, urging that I attend. The invitation came from the alumni committee, comprised of all the kids I would have graduated with had I stayed.

My stomach was in knots that night, too. But I forced myself to go, and I'm so glad I did. To my amazement, everyone seemed genuinely happy to see me. They came up to me and began talking at once, expressing how delighted they were that I had come. Everyone from those years at Holy Ascension was there—Jo Ellen, Terry, Eddie, Greg—all the kids who had once made me cry myself to sleep were now standing before me, laughing *with* me, instead of *at* me.

I'll never forget what happened next. The entire class gathered around me. "Jodee, even though you never graduated with us, we've never forgotten you and we wanted to tell you we're sorry for how we treated you," Eddie said.

"We never hated you. We just didn't understand you. You were always so willing to take a stand and it made us really uncomfortable," Jo Ellen explained. "We've heard what you've done with your life and we're really proud of you. We wanted to tell you this, and that's why we invited you tonight."

For a moment, I was speechless. My mind couldn't wrap itself around what was happening. Before I could gather my thoughts, Greg and Eddie asked if I would sing "Over the Rainbow" for old time's sake. I couldn't understand why they'd want me to perform without music or a microphone. I thought they were kidding, but their faces told a different story. Then, suddenly, I understood. If I sang "Over the Rainbow" to them, it would be a sign of forgiveness, and a reminder of the happy moments of friendship I had once shared with them before the rift between us. Knowing I had to do this, I cleared my throat and began to sing. I sang from my heart, my voice clear and strong. When

I was finished, everyone applauded.

You'd *think* that after all that, this would be a cakewalk for me now—but it's not. A moment ago, I thought I saw someone walking toward my car. Rather than talk with whoever it was, I crouched down in the driver's seat so it would look as if no one was in the car. I'm still so afraid to face Jacklyn and A.J. and all the others who made my life miserable for so many years. They probably don't even remember half of what they did to me. In their minds, they were just kids being kids. But to me and all the other outcasts like me, it was like being castrated. They took something vital from us. It's taken me my whole adult life to get it back, and I'm afraid that if I see my classmates, all those bad memories will come flooding back, and this time I won't be able to shake off the ill effects.

The happy memories of my grammar school reunion quickly fade as images of being kicked and spit at in high school flash through my mind like videotapes. I thought I had escaped the past's grip on me. Foolishly, I believed that being successful as an adult had somehow erased all traces of my "misfitness." As far as the outside world is concerned, it probably has. Yet, inside my own heart, I'm not so sure.

Several years ago, my business partner and I coproduced a celebrity softball game for charity with Styx, my favorite rock band. I never get insecure or uncomfortable around famous people, because working with them is part of my job. But I was nervous about meeting Styx because I loved the band so much when I was young. Would the media I'd invited show up on time to interview them? Would they pose for pictures as promised? Should I let them mingle at the game or would they rather be whisked away to a private trailer? Would they like me?

It was the last question that made me anxious. Yet, what I experienced that afternoon, which was successful on all counts, was nothing compared to the fear and insecurity I'm experiencing right now.

Slowly, I discover my resolve. I check my face in the rear-view mirror. Next, I step out of the car, and move gingerly toward the front of the hotel. When I arrive at the entrance to the ballroom, I open the door a crack and peek inside.

The room is grand and ornate. There are blue-and-gold ribbons and streamers hanging from the ceilings. There are bulletin boards full of photos, and display tables with old yearbooks and other memorabilia. A D.J. is playing a mix from the *Grease* soundtrack. I take a deep breath and go inside, humming the melody from "Over the Rainbow" to myself, trying to recapture how I felt the last time I sang it.

A group of women are talking by the check-in table. When they see me, one of them runs up to me, smiling, and then embraces me. It's Jacklyn. Dressed in light brown suede pants and a buckskin blazer, she's barely aged since high school. I am so surprised by her warm reception that I nearly lose my balance.

"Jodee, it's so good to see you!" she says with real sincerity.

"It's great to see you, too," I say. Half of me wants to ask her why she was so mean to me in high school and if she remembers some of the things she did to me. The other part of me wants to forget all that and simply enjoy this moment and how it feels to finally have her acceptance. I decide to go with the latter. "What are you up to? Are you married? Do you have kids?" I ask.

"I've been married for ten years and have three little girls. I love being a mom—I never thought I could love something so much. What about you? Did you ever marry?"

"I've basically been married to my career. I got into publishing after college."

"I heard you've written a couple of books and that you just finished another one," Jacklyn says. "Everybody's talking about it!"

For a moment, I can barely speak. "Yes," I reply, a little embarrassed. "It's called *Please Stop Laughing at Me*, and it will be out next year."

"What's it about?" she asks.

"It's about school bullying," I answer.

"That's such an important subject," she comments.

"It's inspired by things I went through in school," I say, watching her face to see if she shows any signs of remembering the past.

"Am I in it?" she asks sheepishly.

"I didn't use any real names. I didn't write it to hurt anyone—I wrote it because I don't want other teens feeling like I did at that age."

"That's really something," she says. "If there's anything I can do to help you with this book, let me know."

I fight back tears because I'm so grateful for her support and kindness. At the same time, I am overwhelmed by sadness. It suddenly strikes me that perhaps we could have been buddies in school . . .

As Jacklyn makes her way to the bar, suddenly—out of the corner of my eye—I see *her*. She looks exactly the same as she did in high school. A wave of nausea sweeps over me. My palms sweat. "Hi, A.J." *Please God, let her like me.*

"Jodee, I'm so glad you came!" A.J. says. *Am I hearing correctly? I know there's a condition called Hysterical Blindness that can be brought on by intense stress. Is Hysterical Deafness possible too?*

"I was hoping you'd show up. I hear you're writing books—that's really something. We're all so proud of you," she says, reaching over to give my hand a squeeze.

"Thank you," is all I can manage to say. *This can't be happening. First Jacklyn, now A.J. These girls couldn't stand me in school. They humiliated me every chance they had. What has happened to these people's memories? I must have stepped into some strange episode of* The Twilight Zone.

"What are you doing these days?" I ask her.

"I'm divorced and work in sports marketing," she says. "I don't have any kids. What about you?"

"I'm still single. I've pretty much put all my time into my career," I reply. "I'd like to meet someone, though, and have a family. I'm getting tired of working so much."

"Yeah, but just think of the things you've accomplished! I doubt anyone else in this room is writing books and working with famous people. You should be so proud of yourself."

"I was really scared to come tonight," I admit.

"Why? Everyone always liked you in school," she recalls.

I can no longer contain my amazement. "A.J., I was the outcast at Samuels. I was such a misfit. Don't you remember?"

"You're freaking me out," she says. "Maybe other people made fun of you, but I was never mean to you. I was always nice to you. I honestly liked you."

I realize that it's pointless to make her recall events that occurred more than twenty years ago. In her mind, she and her friends were just "kids being kids." "It was a long time ago, and I understand that maybe you don't remember . . . but A.J., you guys acted like you hated me back then. Why?"

"We were all mean back in high school, I guess," she answers. "It must have been so hard for you. That's probably why you're successful now, because you had to overcome so much. I'm so sorry."

"You know, when we were in high school, I idolized you and Jacklyn. I wanted to *be you*. But I didn't know how to fit in like everyone else. And, yet, maybe if it hadn't been for you and the other kids at Samuels who gave me a hard time, I wouldn't have achieved some of the things I have. The truth is, I still look up to you guys. Standing here right now talking to you, there's a part of me deep inside that's thrilled you finally like me."

A.J. looks down and just shakes her head. "I was scared about coming tonight, too," she admits.

"You? You and Jacklyn were the most popular girls in our class."

"A lot has happened to me since high school. I'm not the same confident person I was then. I pretended a lot."

Right now, all I want to do is hug her. I never would have imagined that the girl I once fantasized about hurting would one day be a woman I'd wish were my sister.

"Later tonight, a bunch of us are going to Skinny Jim's

Bar," A.J. says. "Why don't you hang out with us? I know the offer is a little late, but better late than never, right?" she asks, grinning.

Finally, the dream I've been holding onto for so long is coming true. "I'd love to," I respond, beaming.

After making plans to hook up later at Skinny Jim's, I walk over to the bar and order a glass of white wine. As I'm waiting for my drink, I feel a gentle tap on my shoulder. "Hi, Jodee!" I look behind me. "Noreen! Oh, my God, you look amazing."

Impeccably dressed in a pale pink silk suit, her hair done in a French twist, Noreen doesn't remotely resemble the girl I knew in high school. Vibrant and energetic, she talks animatedly about her life. "After graduation, I floundered for a while, then decided to take a few business courses. I discovered I had a real knack for business. I'm vice president of a small insurance company here in town."

"That's great!" I exclaim. "I'm thrilled to hear you're doing well."

"Did you ever marry?" she inquires.

"No, too busy with my career," I respond. "You?"

"Five years ago," she says. "He's wonderful. We have a toddler at home. He's babysitting tonight, though. He's patient with my career, which is important to me. Speaking of careers, I heard you were writing a book about us. I remember what high school was like for you. It was awful for me, too. I don't want my daughter to live through that kind of hell. If there's anything I can ever do to help you with your book, just call me," she offers.

"Thank you," I reply, touched. We chat a bit more, and

then exchange telephone numbers, promising to get together soon.

This night is turning out to be so much different than I expected. I'm discovering that even though so many of the people here tonight caused me pain when we were kids, I actually like who they've become as adults.

Though most of the old football players are starting to look middle-aged, I can't resist the urge to flirt with them, especially Mark, the former captain of the team. He and Clark see me scoping them out, and they come over.

"Jodee, you look great," Mark says, looking me up and down and giving me a warm hug—a little bit *too* warm.

"Thanks. I waited so long to hear you say that," I reply. "Are you married? Do you have kids?"

"Remember Nadia, the head cheerleader? I married her and we have four children."

"What kind of work do you do?"

"I'm an accountant. I have a small firm not far from here. I hear you're doing really well. What's this about a book you're writing on school bullying?"

"News travels fast," I respond, smiling. "It's based on my own experiences back in school. Don't worry—I've changed everyone's names."

As Mark and I are talking, Nadia comes over. She's still pretty. Dressed in black pants and an angora sweater, the added pounds of motherhood have softened her features.

"What have you been doing with yourself since graduation?" she asks, the tone of her voice cool. She saw the look on her husband's face when he embraced me, so she's now watching us like a hawk.

"I went to school in New York, then got into public relations and publishing," I answer. "I live on the East Coast now. Mark tells me you guys are married and have four kids. I think it's terrific that you were high school sweethearts and have stayed together. It's so romantic."

"I don't know how romantic life is anymore," she jokes, poking Mark gently in the ribs.

"Ouch," he says, giving her a gentle pinch.

Though they appear to be the perfect couple, I see a restlessness beneath their playful veneer.

"Honey, I'm famished," she says, possessively putting her arm around Mark's waist. The message behind the gesture is clear. "We'll see you later, Jodee," she says through slightly clenched teeth. Though I should be a little insulted by Nadia's chilly behavior toward me, I can't help but feel a small sense of satisfaction. Her husband—the same guy who years earlier used to tell me again and again that I was an ugly dog—is now flirting with me and making his cheerleader wife jealous. I'm ashamed to admit it, but it feels great!

As the evening progresses, my confidence steadily grows. My former classmates are going out of their way to include me in the group, as if, unconsciously, they're trying to make up for hurting me. People are asking me to pose for photos with them, and several of the guys have invited me to dance with them. A couple of the football players actually competed with each other over who would stand next to me in the reunion photo. I feel like I'm Cinderella at the ball. This is the best night of my life.

Many of my former classmates aren't at the reunion, but have submitted their bios for the reunion booklet. It

seems as if some of their lives have stood still since graduation; as if they peaked in high school. Others have been successful; a few are still searching for the right career or
spouse. Jim is an accountant and lives in a small town in
rural Wyoming. Greg is married with three kids and works
as a lumberjack out west. Rickie is an insurance salesman.
Emily is a full-time homemaker. Kim and Jason have had it
rough: Kim is a single mom, married and divorced twice,
who's struggling to make ends meet; Jason is battling a
drinking problem. He's had his license suspended for DUIs.

The one person I haven't seen here tonight is Sharon. I
wonder what's become of her. Annie is doing fine, but couldn't
make the reunion because she's eight months pregnant.

"You turned out to be a real beauty," says a familiar
voice behind me.

"Tyler, it's great to see you!" This guy teased and humiliated me in high school, but my knees still get weak twenty
years later at the sound of his voice.

"I mean it. You look terrific," he says, staring at me.

"Thanks. You do, too," I respond. "You've gotten even
sexier since high school." Do my eyes deceive me, or is Mr.
Cool himself actually blushing?

"When's the last time we saw each other?" Tyler asks.

"It was when you signed my yearbook. Do you
remember what you wrote in it?" I ask. I don't know what
will make me feel worse, if he remembers or if he doesn't.

"What? Did I write something stupid?" he inquires with
a lame grin.

"I can still smell the ink from that big black marker of
yours," I reply, the old anger beginning to rise within me.

"You printed in capital letters 'You'll have to fuck yourself, we hate you, bitch.'"

Tyler's embarrassment is palpable. His face turns bright red.

"You're kidding," he responds. "I actually wrote that?"

"Yes, it's my last memory of high school," I answer.

"God, I'm sorry. I was such a jerk back then . . . so full of myself," he recalls.

"It was a long time ago," I offer. Just then, a petite young blond woman walks over to us, slipping her arm through Tyler's.

"Jodee, this is my wife, Laurie," Tyler says, introducing us.

"It's nice to meet you," she replies, extending her hand. "Would you excuse me for a moment? I need to powder my nose," she says, leaving for the bathroom.

"She seems like a really nice girl," I observe.

"She is, but we're very different people," he says.

"That's too bad. Love is tough to find, easy to lose," I remark.

"There's something I want to tell you," Tyler says. "If I don't do it now, I never will."

"What is it?" I ask.

"Jodee, I knew you had a crush on me in high school. Everybody did. That was the problem. The sad part is that I liked you, too."

Could I have heard him right?

"But I was afraid of what my friends would say if I asked you out, because you were, you know . . ." He stops, unsure if he should continue.

"A *reject*?" I volunteer.

"I wouldn't put it that way," he says.

"It's okay, Tyler, you can say it."

"All right, yes, I didn't ask you out because I was worried my crowd would disown me if they knew I liked you," he admits. "That's why I wrote those awful things in your yearbook and teased you so much."

"Then you did remember about the yearbook?" I observe, smiling.

"Yeah, I remembered."

"Tyler, thank you for telling me all this. You'll never know how much it helps me to hear it."

"I should have said something a long time ago," he says. Then, he kisses me gently on the cheek and walks away to find his wife. As I turn toward the buffet table, a gorgeous man approaches me. I can't quite place who he is, so I squint to read his nametag. "You probably don't remember me, but we were in biology class together," he says, smiling. "My name is Mitch. I sat next to Clark and Tyler in Ms. Raine's class."

"Oh, my God, I remember you! *I didn't remember him when I was writing the book, but boy, oh boy, do I remember him now.* You used to hang out with Jacklyn and A.J. Wow, have you filled out since high school," I observe. "I honestly didn't recognize you."

"That's okay. You look a lot different, too," he says, staring into my eyes.

What are the chances that I would meet a great guy at my high school reunion? I'm so delighted, I could burst out into song. "Stay cool," I tell myself. "I think this guy likes you."

He takes my hand and leads me onto the dance floor and we dance for hours. Afterward, we join everyone at Skinny Jim's, where we drink and laugh and enjoy each other's company. "Everyone, I'd like to make a toast," I say, raising my glass. "To our twentieth reunion and to the people we've become!

As we clink glasses, I realize that the terror is gone forever. Not only am I no longer frightened or angry at my former classmates, I am interested in getting to know them better. My mind drifts for a moment to the senior prom. I'm finally experiencing the magic I longed to feel back on that night. As Mitch wraps his arm around me, suddenly, a part of me that's been dark and closed for so long opens up and I can feel sunlight pouring in. Everyone at this table is human and vulnerable, the same as me. They can't hurt me anymore. I think we may finally even become friends. Relief washes over me. I reach inside my purse, pull out an old Bonnie Bell lip-gloss, and remove the cap. Though this lip-gloss is more than ten years old, remarkably, it still retains its moisture. But then, remarkable has been the norm tonight.

I apply the sweet, familiar substance to my lips. Then, I take a long, deep breath and do something I never thought I'd have the courage to do—but I know that I must in order to be free. I *let go*. I let go of all the hurt and anger that has held me secretly hostage all these years—the rage over tears shed and words never spoken. I let go of the bitterness and sadness, the loneliness that has haunted me, and the stale, unfulfilled daydreams of my youth. I close my eyes and envision the images of everyone who was ever kind to me while I was growing up—my parents, grandparents, my aunts and cousins, Dr. Arnold, Annie and her gang of caring misfits, and Niko and my loving friends in Santorini. These people held me up when I needed it most and I thank God for them.

I feel as if I'm floating now. The weight I've been carrying inside me for so long has been lifted. I slowly open my eyes and smile at my former classmates sitting before me. I can finally forgive them . . . and myself.

Author's Note

It's surprising what we appreciate when we're adults. When I was a teenager, if someone had told me that one day, I would look back and be grateful for the hell I was going through; that it would make me a better person when I grew up, I would have thought they were crazy. Now, as a mature woman, I can't believe this has actually happened.

I never take it for granted when someone honors me with their friendship. I also stand by my friends no matter what, because I know how awful it is when someone who's supposed to be on your side turns her back on you.

When I was in my late twenties, my breasts started to lose their shape, as the Mayo Clinic predicted they would due to the natural maturing process of the body. A few years ago, I finally had the second breast surgery. Dr. Arnold, the wonderful surgeon who performed the first procedure, did the operation. That man is a true miracle worker. My chest is beautiful now and he says I'll never need surgery again.

I've also suffered losses along the way. My dad had rheumatic fever as a child and his kidneys failed when he was fifty-eight years old. My mother and I both still miss him every day. My grandparents and Aunt Evie passed away of old age in the 1990s. Niko, the boy who gave me back my dignity one summer in Santorini and who remained my close friend for more than two decades, was killed in a tragic accident during the writing of this book. All these people live in my heart.

I would not wish my early life on anyone, but it is my life. It's a large part of who I am now. The pain I went through as a teen strengthened me and taught me the truth of that wonderful adage about doing unto others as you would wish them to do unto you. I have discovered that doing what you love actually enhances your chances for success, and treating people as you want to be treated is a good way to make friends and do business. The ethical standards of my parents, although so difficult to honor during my troubled youth, serve me well as a woman happy in her profession, blessed with loving friends.

Professional Biography of Jodee Blanco

J odee Blanco is a leading public relations specialist in the book publishing and entertainment industries, with fifteen *New York Times* bestsellers to her credit, including five at number one, and dozens of regional bestsellers (*The L.A. Times, The Washington Post, The Chicago Tribune*).

Some of those titles include: *Secrets About Men Every Woman Should Know* by acclaimed relationship expert Dr. Barbara DeAngelis; *On the Outside Looking In* by Michael Reagan, former President Reagan's son; *The Duke of Flatbush* by renowned Brooklyn Dodger Duke Snider; *Healing the Shame That Binds You* by self-help expert and therapist John Bradshaw; and *Out of Bounds* by football hall-of-famer, movie star, and activist Jim Brown; among many others.

She has represented many newsmakers and personalities, such as: bestselling author, writer, actor, and director Carl Reiner; the executive producers of the Emmy Award–winning hit series *Seinfeld*, George Shapiro and Howard West; bestselling author Bob Zmuda, executive producer of *Man on the Moon*, the Golden Globe–winning film about performance artist Andy Kaufman, starring Jim Carrey and Danny DeVito and directed by Oscar winner Milos Forman, which Blanco also represented; Comic Relief, the celebrated charity for the homeless that airs live broadcasts on HBO with hosts Whoopie Goldberg, Billy Crystal, and Robin Williams; *New York Times* bestselling author and Hollywood legend Mickey Rooney; and the former Director of Middle East Operations for the CIA, "America's Real-Life James Bond," Eric Jordan; among many others.

A decade ago, Jodee Blanco founded her first company, Blanco & Peace, with veteran film publicist Lissy Peace. During her years as president of Blanco & Peace, Ms. Blanco developed and executed innovative campaigns for many authors that redefined the possibilities for publicizing books.

Some of those *New York Times* bestselling authors include: Dave Pelzer, who debuted on the *New York Times* bestseller list with his first book, *A Child Called "It,"* then made the list a second time with the sequel *The Lost Boy* (both books remained on the *Times* list for years); science fiction writer Kevin Anderson, known for his internationally successful prequels to the popular *Dune* and *Star Wars* series; and the literary estate of Daphne du Maurier, author of the legendary *Rebecca*; among dozens of others.

She has worked with leading publishing houses, which include Warner Books; Simon & Schuster; The Free Press; Dell; Delacorte; MacMillan; Avon; Morrow; Atlantic Monthly Press; John Wiley; HarperCollins; McGraw-Hill; Little, Brown and Company; Carroll & Graf; Houghton Mifflin; and Henry Holt.

In addition to her passion for publishing projects, her

lifelong love and reverence for old Hollywood fuel her continued desire to work with the luminaries who have shaped the entertainment industry. Ms. Blanco contributed to the success of projects that have been near and dear to some of these legendary hearts. She was the catalyst for the groundbreaking deal between Mickey Rooney and his publisher that facilitated Rooney's debut as a novelist.

Ms. Blanco has also developed and managed publicity and promotions strategies for a broad spectrum of international projects, including: a twelve-acre theme park in Thailand; the largest privately sponsored Civil War memorial event in the history of the United States; the World Expo in Taejon, Korea; a book launch in the nation's capital that brought together an illustrious assembly of ambassadors, CIA officers, political leaders, and a former top-ranking member of the KGB that garnered extensive coverage in *The Washington Post* and other D.C. media, who proclaimed it a landmark event.

Ms. Blanco is a faculty member at New York University's Center for Publishing and the University of Chicago. She is a frequent guest speaker at industry events like BookExpo America, and seminars sponsored by such entities as *Publishers Weekly*, the American Booksellers Association, the American Society of Authors and Journalists, and Women in Publishing. She is the author of *The Complete Guide to Book Publicity* and coauthor of the award-winning book *The Evolving Woman*.

Ms. Blanco reads, writes, and speaks fluent Greek. She splits her time between Manhattan, Chicago, and Pennsylvania.

Resources

No one should have to endure being teased, bullied, or abused. Cruelty violates a person's sense of self and others. If you or someone you know—perhaps your son, daughter, student, or a friend—is being bullied at school, you can help. Listen to them. Let them know they are not alone in their struggle. Be compassionate, supportive, and strong.

There are many organizations expert in dealing with troubled teens. Outlined below are three specific recommended resources.

- KidsPeace National Center for Kids Overcoming Crisis
General Web site: *www.kidspeace.org*
Teen Web site: *www.teencentral.net*
Crisis hotline: 1-800-334-4543

- National Suicide Prevention Hotline
1-800-SUICIDE

• The Blue Pages of your local phone book is probably one of the most comprehensive resources available. It lists regional and national crisis hotlines, as well as self-help organizations and support groups in your local area.

• BULLYING ONLINE
www.bullying.co.uk
This Web site, out of the U.K., features extensive information on the subject, including advice for parents, students, and teachers; legal advice; helpful links and tips; and ideas for school projects to stop bullying.